BUDGET-FRIENDLY COLLEGE COOKBOOK

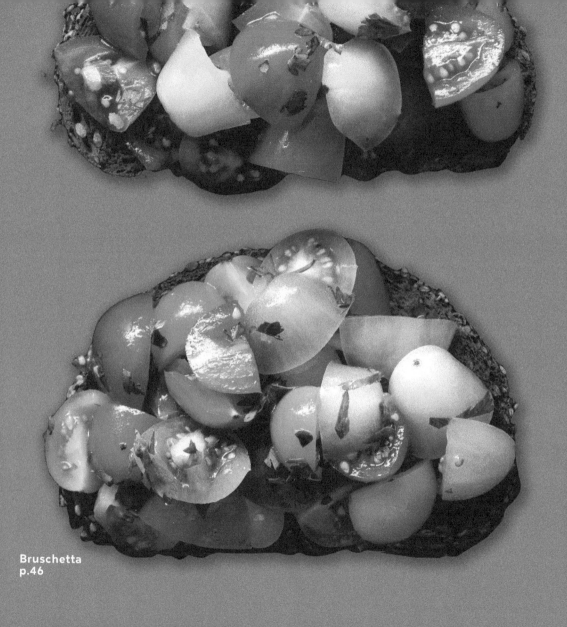

Bruschetta
p.46

BUDGET-FRIENDLY

★ ★ ★

COLLEGE COOKBOOK

Sara Lundberg

EATING WELL WITH LIMITED
SPACE, STORAGE, AND SAVINGS

ROCKRIDGE
PRESS

Interior & Cover Designer: Francesca Pacchini
Art Producer: Janice Ackerman
Editor: Daniel Grogan, Marjorie DeWitt
Production Editor: Rachel Taenzler
Cover Photography: Nachos: © Olga Miltsova/shutterstock; mug: © 2020 Paul Sirisalee.
ii: Pixel Stories/Stocksy; vi: Darren Muir; x: Dimitrije Tanaskovic/Stocksy;
xii: Gillian Vann/Stocksy; p. 25: icons/shutterstock; p. 26: Paul Sirisalee;
p. 37: MARTÍ SANS/Stocksy; p. 40: Marija Vidal; p. 52: StockFood/Flores Avalos Maricruz; p. 82: StockFood/Stacy Ventura; p. 112: Marija Vidal.

ISBN: Print 978-1-64611-674-4 | eBook 978-1-64611-675-1

R0

TO MY FOUR CHILDREN, WITHOUT WHOM THIS BOOK
WOULD HAVE BEEN COMPLETED TWO YEARS EARLIER.

Homemade Hummus
p.48

CONTENTS

CHAPTER 4:

CHAPTER 5:

CHAPTER 6: FOR THE SWEET TOOTH 113

Spiced Popcorn
p.42

INTRODUCTION

One of the things most people take away from college, besides student debt, is a habitual dining routine. As a student on campus, you may lack a ton of resources, which can lead to poor eating habits that result in gaining that notorious Freshman 15. You may also gain or lose too much weight depending on how you cope with the stresses of college life. But the biggest factor in poor nutrition is the cost of food. The ironic thing is fast food costs way more than meals you make at home. Homemade meals, as you probably know, also tend to be healthier.

If you want to make your own meals, the one thing that may get in your way is having the time and the space to cook. Luckily, you can turn just about any space into a kitchen with the right accessories. As you will see with the recipes in this book, you can reuse a lot of ingredients and make simple, safe, delicious, high-quality foods in a short amount of time.

Using the recipes in this book, you will stay fed and happy, and even impress your guests with your resourcefulness. The tips and meal suggestions you'll find here are a good start to a healthy and low-cost lifestyle that will benefit you throughout your college years and beyond. So gather up as many condiment packets as you can at your local burger joint, because you won't be back for a while.

Rosemary-
Garlic
Potatoes
p.50

1

Cooking on a Tiny Budget in a Tiny Kitchen

College life is full of challenges. Cooking your own meals is one of the exciting ones, but there are two obstacles to overcome: money and space. In this chapter you'll learn how you can cook on a very small budget and how you can put your limited space to good use.

TOOLS OF THE TRADE

You can make any space work for you, no matter how bare-bones your kitchen area may be. Most of the suggestions and recipes provided in this book assume that you don't have much to work with, although there are some recipes that call for a larger cooking environment, whether it's a shared kitchen or a modest kitchen of your own (for those who are lucky enough to live in apartment-style dorms). The key to getting started is selecting the most useful tools. Before you begin to cook, gather necessary tools like kitchen scissors, a can opener, whisk, spatula, knife, measuring cups—and don't forget sponges and towels for cleaning up a mess. A clean work space will help the cooking process go much more smoothly.

THE *ESSENTIAL* ESSENTIALS

You don't need fancy gizmos or super specific one-trick-pony instruments to fill up your junk drawer. Get the best return on your investment by sticking with only the necessities that are used throughout this book. The more equipment you can easily store and have on hand for cooking, the better. The following list contains the best essential appliances and tools to help you get the most delicious meals out of the least amount of space. You may not have to purchase all of these things, but I do strongly recommend that you bring as many of the following items as possible into your dorm (or makeshift) kitchen. This book contains a variety of useful recipes, regardless of how many or which appliances you are able to get your hands on.

- Mini refrigerator (or larger if your situation allows it)
- Microwave
- Electric hot plate
- Slow cooker
- Skillet
- Small pot or saucepan
- Microwave-safe plates
- Microwave-safe bowls
- Microwave-safe mugs
- Food storage containers
- Plastic cutting board

- Chopping knife
- Forks
- Spoons
- Mixing bowls
- Measuring cups
- Kitchen scissors
- Meat thermometer
- Can opener
- Cooking spoon
- Spatula
- Strainer

Please keep in mind that your university may have different guidelines for what is permissible in a dorm. Be aware of any restrictions as you piece together your "kitchen" area. Even with some pretty harsh restrictions, you should have no problem keeping these essentials in a storage box on an easily accessible shelf.

WHEN YOU'VE GOT A KITCHEN

Supposing you have your own kitchen or at least access to a communal one, there are other items that can take your cooking to the next level. You don't need these items like you need the utensils and equipment mentioned on page 3. However, when you have the space or the opportunity to add more to your arsenal, you should always take it. These items will come in handy if you have extra counter space, an oven, and/or a larger refrigerator.

- Baking sheet
- Casserole dish
- Large pot
- Mixing bowls (various sizes)
- Colander
- Spice rack
- Salt and pepper shakers

GOOD TO HAVE, IF YOU CAN

Some kitchen items are not essential but sure are nice to have. If you have the luxury of storage space and can borrow any of these, do so. If borrowing is not an option and you really think one or more of these items would enhance your life, check for them at your local thrift store or look for used models online.

- Food processor
- Blender
- Coffee maker
- Pressure cooker

SMART SHOPPING

The size of your living space is definitely a factor in how you cook, but so is your budget. Part of the appeal of cooking for yourself is saving money, right? As with any investment, cooking for yourself may require more upfront capital, but you don't have to wait long to see your returns. You also don't have to pay as much as you think if you implement some smart shopping skills.

If you have limited cold storage space (for instance, if you're sharing a refrigerator with other people or only have a mini refrigerator), make sure you are mindful of portion sizes when you shop so that you don't spend money on food that you can't finish or keep. Just because you have an oven to work with doesn't mean you should spend money on ingredients that you don't have room for. Most of the recipes in this book make single servings, but in chapter 5, you'll find some meals you can prepare for friends and special company.

BUY IN SEASON. There are several practical reasons why you should buy fresh fruits and vegetables when they are in season. Frozen veggies may be difficult for you to store if you don't have a regular-size freezer, and they often don't taste as good as their fresh counterparts. Plus, in-season produce is much less expensive and more flavorful and nutritious than out-of-season options that have to be shipped hundreds or thousands of miles to the grocery store. A quick internet search will help you determine when various fruits and vegetables are in season in your area and whether there's a nearby farmers' market where you can purchase these items at even more affordable prices.

CHOOSE THE BEST GROCERY STORE FOR YOU. Every grocery store has its advantages and disadvantages. One store may have consistently low prices across the board but not the lowest price for everything. Another store may have great deals only for club members. Online stores may feature a wider variety of items with the trade-offs of shipping costs and delays—and inconsistencies in the quality of fresh ingredients. If you're going to be cooking for yourself on a regular basis, try out a few different grocery stores to find the one that best fits your needs.

MAKE A LIST. It's easy to make purchases based on price or buy a lot of things you like without having an actual plan. There's no need to create a spreadsheet with multitiered meal plans, but you should have a purpose in mind for every item you buy to avoid wasting money. Taking just a few minutes to sit down and consider what you really need from the store will make you more focused when you get there.

USE COUPONS. Now, with in-store and third-party apps offering regular discounts, it's easier than ever to save money using coupons. Planning your meals around the promotions advertised on your grocery store's website, app, or membership rewards program is a smart way to save money and enjoy delicious, homemade food all week long.

COMPARE UNIT PRICES. In some cases, it makes sense to choose the sizes and brands of food items based on the price per unit. If your grocery store labels products with their price per ounce, use this information to shop for the brand or size that offers the lowest price per ounce for that item.

KNOW WHAT TO BUY IN BULK. Buying in bulk can be tempting, especially if your friend has a membership to a warehouse store like Costco or Sam's Club (and a car, for that matter). It's not always a great deal to buy large quantities, though, even if the price per unit is significantly discounted. Be careful not to pay too much for products you may not use or have the space to store.

WATCH OUT FOR END-OF-THE-AISLE DISPLAYS. Grocery stores will often place items on the end of the aisle to make you think they are on sale. Sometimes this space is used for actual promotions, but always check the price before you overpay for a product because of its enticing display.

CHECK EXPIRATION DATES AND LABEL OPENED CONTAINERS. When you're shopping, always check the use-by or purchase-by date of a food before you place it in your cart. Then, when you open a container of perishable food (like yogurt, milk, or hummus), add 10 days to the date you opened it, and label it with that date. (The expiration date is only good when the container remains sealed.) For extra efficiency, try to organize your refrigerator with the newest foods in the back and the ones closest to expiring in the front. That way, you're less likely to hang on to expired foods, which take up precious space, can start to smell (depending on what it is), and which—worst-case scenario—you might accidentally eat if you forget when you opened them.

USE EVERYTHING YOU BUY. Food is perishable, and it does way more good in your body than it does crammed in the back of the refrigerator. So, the next time you catch yourself thinking that you should save a food item for some future date, consider the irony that trying to conserve food can often lead to spoilage and waste. Throughout the recipe chapters, you'll find tips on how to use leftover ingredients in interesting ways so that none of the food you buy ends up in the trash can.

WHICH SPICES DO YOU *REALLY* NEED?

One easy way to enhance the flavor of your food is with an assortment of go-to herbs and spices. Building your pantry spices may seem like an investment, but it's worth it! Dried spices will last for up to three years, and they can be used to liven up just about any snack or meal. You can find an array of dried herbs and spices in your grocery store's baking aisle. Look for store brands, which are usually the cheapest, and choose the ones that you know you'll use the most. Here's a list of the most frequently used spices in this book, to get you started:

- Table salt
- Black pepper
- Garlic powder
- Onion powder
- Cinnamon

INGREDIENTS TO STOCK IN YOUR CABINET, CLOSET, OR DORMITORY SHELF

No matter how much cooking space you have, you need to have some storage space set aside for nonperishable cooking essentials. Keep your shelf or cabinet stocked with dried spices and a variety of canned foods and inexpensive grains.

DRIED PASTA: Pasta is inexpensive and very convenient. It fills you up, and it can be used with a variety of sauces to achieve different flavors. Pasta comes in many varieties, so you can choose which shapes you prefer or stock up on a few different options for classic combos like macaroni and cheese, spaghetti marinara, or fettuccine alfredo. Pasta is also a long-lasting ingredient, which makes it a perfect staple for your pantry.

BULK RICE: The best thing you can stock your shelf with is a bag of rice. It's a long-lasting ingredient, and because it expands in water, a little goes a long way. Rice is also cheap, and it goes with everything. Whether you create a bowl, a casserole, or a side dish, rice can provide a good foundation for your meal.

INSTANT RAMEN NOODLES: Packaged instant ramen is incredibly inexpensive, but it can be used for more than just a fast, cheap meal. You can enhance ramen in many ways, as you'll see in several recipes. Make sure you have plenty of ramen noodles stocked in your makeshift pantry. Once you learn how simple it is to create meal masterpieces out of these simple packets of dried noodles, there's no going back!

OATS: Save money and enjoy the taste and health benefits of old-fashioned rolled oats by using them to make your own oatmeal. Head to the bulk section of your grocery store to buy only what you need or bulk quantities if you have the space. (Oats can be stored in an airtight container in a cool, dry place for up to two years.) No matter how much you choose to buy, make sure oats get a spot on your shelf, because they are a terrific grain, ideal for breakfast treats like oatmeal, parfaits, and pastries.

CANNED DICED TOMATOES: If you can only keep one canned food in your pantry, closet, or shelf, make it diced tomatoes. Canned tomatoes are versatile and used in all types of recipes, especially Italian- and Mexican-inspired dishes.

CANNED VEGETABLES: Canned vegetables are cheaper than fresh vegetables, and since they are canned at their peak freshness, they contain the same amount of nutrients. Besides being cheaper and just as good for you, canned vegetables last a lot longer than their fresh counterparts. Stock up on your favorites, from carrots to artichokes, and store as much variety as you can so that you can whip up interesting meals and snacks whenever you feel like cooking.

CANNED BEANS: There are all kinds of beans for all kinds of tastes. Canned beans have the same benefits as other canned foods. They last a really long time, and they are high in protein and fiber, which make them a key factor in a nutritious diet. Black beans are great for Southwestern-inspired dishes; chickpeas are delicious in salads and are the key ingredient in hummus. Kidney beans, red beans, and pinto beans are terrific sources of nutrients, too.

CANNED SOUPS: Canned soup is a great meal option when you don't want to cook, but it can also make your cooking so much better. Tomato soup can be used as a base for certain casseroles, skillet meals, and slow-cooker/pressure-cooker recipes. Cream of mushroom soup and cream of celery soup can add moisture and depth of flavor to potentially dry and tasteless dishes. Cream of chicken soup also enhances flavor and reduces dryness and is especially delicious in chicken pot pie, chicken chili, and chicken-and-rice casserole.

CHICKEN BROTH: Combine chicken broth with fresh or frozen veggies and other ingredients to make your own soup, or use it instead of water to cook rice. You can even make mashed potatoes with it. Not only does broth add savory flavor, it's also a great way to add extra protein and nutrients to a dish.

CANNED COCONUT MILK: If you keep a can of coconut milk on hand, you will be prepared for curries and Asian-inspired dishes that rely on the natural sweetness of this ingredient for their distinctive flavor.

SALT: Almost all the recipes in this book instruct you to season with salt to taste. Although it's not essential, salt makes a big difference in flavor.

A note on canned goods: Always check the sell-by or use-by date printed on the can before you buy or open a canned food item. If you open a can of food and do not use it all right away, cover the can with plastic wrap or aluminum foil (or transfer the remaining contents to an airtight container), and refrigerate it for up to two weeks.

NOTHING LASTS FOREVER

Dried spices, canned foods, and other goods may have long shelf lives, but everything expires eventually. Here are the shelf lives of some dry essentials you should keep on hand if you plan to cook regularly for yourself. You can safely buy the longer-lasting ingredients in larger quantities.

Ingredient	Shelf life (stored in an airtight container in a cool, dark place)
FLOUR	3 months
GRANULATED AND BROWN SUGAR	2 years
IODIZED SALT*	5 years
BAKING POWDER	1 year
DRIED RICE	5 years
DRIED PASTA	2 years
OATS	2 years
DRIED SPICES	3 years

*Salt alone does not expire, but additives can limit its potency.

INGREDIENTS TO STOCK IN YOUR FRIDGE

Assuming you have a mini refrigerator in your dorm room, there are some essentials, besides water and *other* beverages, that you should keep stocked. Since you can keep unopened canned fruits, veggies, and beans at room temperature for a very long time, your stocked mini refrigerator will be very dairy-centric. However, there are some other essentials that will make you glad you have refrigerator space.

EGGS: A good source of protein and the foundation of traditional breakfasts, eggs are cheap and versatile. Prepare them any number of ways, and use them in any meal from salads to soufflés.

BUTTER: A key cooking ingredient you should always keep on hand, butter can be used to grease pots and pans and to cook vegetables and meats. It's also an essential component in sauces and baked goods, particularly those that contain flour.

SLICED CHEESE: Unlike block cheese, sliced cheese lies flat and reduces prep time and the need for utensils. It's ideal for sandwiches and melts.

SHREDDED CHEESE: Cheese in this form also reduces prep time and takes up minimal space in the refrigerator. It's ideal for topping salads and one-bowl meals.

YOGURT: Keep a tub of yogurt in the refrigerator for quick, high-protein snacks or to add creaminess to meals.

MILK: Whole milk or 2 percent milk is an essential cooking ingredient. If you have a refrigerator, you should have milk. If you have a small refrigerator, you may have to pay a little more per ounce and get individual milk bottles or cartons at a smaller local retailer.

LETTUCE: This is the starting point for an endless variety of hearty salads. You should have other essential salad ingredients, such as beans and other vegetables, in cans. Tear up some lettuce leaves, add whatever other ingredients you like, and toss them all together in a bowl for an instant healthy meal or side.

SALAD DRESSING: You can use bottled salad dressing for more than salads. It's also great as a marinade for meat and chicken or as a flavor enhancer. Vinaigrettes are very versatile, and blue cheese, ranch, and Thousand Island salad dressings make terrific dipping sauces.

CONDIMENTS: Dedicate a small section of your refrigerator to basic condiments like ketchup, mustard, and mayonnaise, even if they're just packets that you grab from the cafeteria. If you have room, include your favorite barbecue sauce, too.

If You Have More Space . . .

If you have more refrigerator space, you can significantly boost your cooking range and convenience. You can even save more money, because you can reasonably buy larger quantities of items at a reduced price. A larger refrigerator space—whether you have your own or share a full-size refrigerator with other people—is an opportunity to include more fresh fruits, veggies, and even juice in your home-cooked meals. Of course, all of the items on this list can be stored in a mini refrigerator as well, but having a bigger refrigerator means you'll be able to have more of the items on hand.

CHICKEN THIGHS: The best meat you can keep in your refrigerator is chicken. It's good for you and relatively inexpensive. Thigh meat is the cheapest of all the chicken options at the grocery store, and it's very versatile, which means you'll have no trouble cooking the whole package. Whenever you need to add some animal protein to a dish, use chicken thighs.

WHOLE PRECOOKED (ROTISSERIE) CHICKEN: In most supermarkets, you can get a whole rotisserie chicken for pretty cheap. It takes up minimal refrigerator space and can serve you well for several meals if you plan it out right. Leave it whole in the container or carve it up right away for convenience later.

SLICED DELI MEAT: A package of deli meat lies flat and doesn't take up too much space. It's also a key component of sandwiches, which are great go-to meals when you don't have time to cook.

SLICED BREAD: You don't need to store bread in a refrigerator, but refrigeration greatly prolongs its shelf life. If you have the room to store it in the refrigerator, you'll be more likely to get through the whole loaf before it goes bad.

TORTILLAS: These bread alternatives are staples of Mexican-inspired cuisine. Like bread, they last longer when stored in the refrigerator.

PEANUT BUTTER: A good source of protein and essential fats, peanut butter can be used in a variety of creative ways when cooking, but it's especially convenient for quick snacks or sandwiches.

JELLY OR FRUIT PRESERVES: Like peanut butter, jelly is perfect for sandwiches, but it also has a variety of other potential uses in the kitchen. It can serve as a dessert topping or as a key component in making home-made vinaigrettes and sauces.

LEMONS: Sour and bright, lemon is commonly used to add flavor to many different dishes, either on its own as a garnish or in sauces, marinades, and vinaigrettes in the form of juice or zest (grated peel). Lemon pairs well with black pepper.

LIMES: The distinct tartness of lime adds a different bright acidity to food than lemon. It can complement lemony flavor or take your entrée in an entirely different direction. Lime pairs well with chili powder.

BERRIES: Fresh berries are a delicious, healthy, sweet snack filled with antioxidants and other nutrients. They make a nice addition to salads, desserts, and breakfast dishes, or can be served on their own.

FRESH VEGETABLES: Fresh, ready-to-use vegetables are always great to have on hand if you have the cold storage space. Among the top useful veggies are carrots, celery, and onions. When you buy fresh vegetables to store in your refrigerator, be sure to have a plan for them. Vegetables are often purchased with the best intentions but then forgotten about and left to rot. Store tomatoes, potatoes, thick-skinned winter squash, avocados (until they have ripened), and onions at room temperature in a cool, dark place like a closet or bin. Store all other fresh vegetables in the refrigerator.

EMPTY STORAGE CONTAINERS: Here is a useful tip: Reserve room in your refrigerator for future leftovers by using empty containers as spacers.

SCALLIONS!

One of the most versatile fresh flavor enhancers you can keep in your kitchen space is scallions. They have a nice oniony flavor that goes with anything savory, and you don't even have to refrigerate them. As long as you have the root, you can keep scallions in water, and they will continue to grow!

FIVE TIPS FOR FRUGAL LIVING

Time and money were always the two biggest challenges for me when I wanted to cook my own meals in my dorm room. The money part was what really threw me because when I found out how much I was spending on convenient meals, I knew there had to be a better way. I found that I could stretch my food budget with better planning and by using food I already had at home. Here's some advice to help you get the most out of a meager food budget.

1. **Find a frugal source.** Avoid choosing convenience over affordability. Find out where to go for the items you pay for most often. Keep your eyes open for deals, coupons, and rewards programs.

2. **Stretch your grocery budget with dried beans.** Though you might be drawn to the convenience of canned beans, dried beans take up less room in your makeshift pantry, are super cheap, and are incredibly versatile and easy to prepare (as long as you have a

pot and a hot plate). Get yourself a bag of whatever kind of bean you like, and it will last you for several different meals. For best results, soak the dried beans overnight in water, then drain them, put them in your pot, and cover with fresh water. Cook until the beans are tender (this could take anywhere from 45 minutes to 2 hours, depending on the type of bean).

3. **Don't skip paid meals.** A meal plan, if reasonably priced, is a great way to supplement your own cooking and keep yourself satisfied and well nourished, as long as you remember to take full advantage of it. You don't want to finish out the semester with hundreds of dollars remaining on your plan's account, especially if the money doesn't roll over.

4. **Shop before you're hungry.** Don't wait until you are hungry to go grocery shopping—that's when you should be cooking. Know what you want to make and make a list of practical and necessary items before you go shopping for ingredients.

5. **Mooch around campus.** Often, clubs on campus will host special events that include a spread of complimentary food. Scour the bulletin boards and listen for word about any scheduled events where free food will be served.

LIVING FIRE-, CUT-, AND DISEASE-FREE (AT LEAST FROM FOOD)

Always follow these food- and cooking-related safety precautions, as well as any additional rules you are expected to follow in your dorm room, apartment, or house:

KEEP KNIVES SHARP. With a sharp knife, you can chop ingredients with ease using very little pressure. Dull knives require you to use sawing motions and press down harder on foods, which results in less presentable food, poor accuracy, and a higher likelihood of personal injury.

KEEP YOUR COOKING SPACE CLEAN. A clean work area promotes a hazard-free environment.

DATE YOUR OPENED CONTAINERS. The expiration date on a sealed food container is only accurate if the product is unopened. Once you open any food container, you should usually use it up or throw it out after 7 to 10 days. This is especially true of items that require refrigeration after opening.

KEEP TRACK OF REFRIGERATOR TEMPERATURE. Don't let the refrigerator temperature rise above 40°F or your food will start to spoil.

UNPLUG APPLIANCES AFTER USE. When appliances are not in use, remove them from the power supply. You may not have to worry about electric bills just yet, but keeping appliances unplugged can prevent fires.

WASH YOUR HANDS. Always wash your hands with soap and water before cooking any food. Use warm water, and scrub up to your elbows for about 15 seconds before rinsing.

CHECK THE INTERNAL TEMPERATURE OF COOKED MEATS. Keep a meat thermometer handy for checking the internal temperature of any meat you cook to avoid harmful bacteria.

WEAR THE RIGHT CLOTHES. In chemistry lab, you remove loose clothing and jewelry to avoid accidents. Cooking is chemistry, so the same rules apply.

USE ANTIBACTERIAL CLEANERS. Clean your countertops and everything food touches with antibacterial cleaner to avoid contamination and prevent foodborne illnesses.

KEEP SAFETY EQUIPMENT CLOSE BY. Be sure you know where the nearest fire extinguisher is, and keep a first aid kit close at hand in case your safety preparedness and prevention methods are unsuccessful.

EATING HEALTHY ON A BUDGET: AVOIDING THE FRESHMAN 15

The first year of college is rough. As you feed your head with knowledge, you may start to feel like it's all going straight to your gut. That's because it takes practice and determination to incorporate the right foods in your daily diet. It is all too easy to slip into bad habits, especially when dealing with so many new responsibilities and emerging life events. Even if you're not tempted to stress eat, it can sometimes feel like you don't have the time or the money to eat right. But that's where you're wrong! All you need to do to eat healthy on a budget is focus a little bit more attention on that goal. Shop smart, and put just a little bit of work in so that you can build better eating habits. Include a healthy balance of protein, fiber, vitamins, and minerals in your regular meals. Concentrate more on eating good things than on attempting to cut back on foods you shouldn't eat. That's how you fill up on the right stuff and break bad habits.

ABOUT THE RECIPES

Once you get into the mind-set that you want to cook at home, you need a leg up in order to see it through. This book will provide you with great-tasting recipes for various occasions. They're nutritious, easy to make, and, best of all, cheap. You can quickly and easily make these recipes in even the smallest kitchens using the right equipment, and you'll only need to spend about $5 or less per serving in ingredients. Use this book to learn fast and easy recipes and get inspired to try some things on your own. Up ahead are delicious breakfast ideas, shareable entrées, tantalizing desserts, and so much more. As you prepare these meals using the simple methods and smart shopping techniques provided, you will eat well and gain confidence instead of unwanted pounds. Each recipe will have icons to let you know if a toaster, toaster oven, hot plate, microwave, blender, or slow cooker is needed. If none of these symbols appear, then none of the appliances are required.

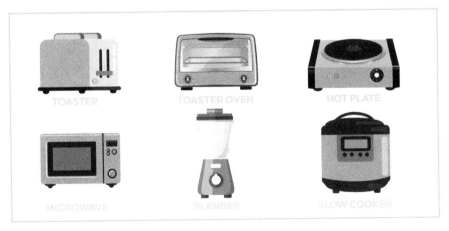

TOASTER   TOASTER OVEN   HOT PLATE

MICROWAVE   BLENDER   SLOW COOKER

Vanilla Yogurt
and Berry Parfait p.30

Big and Small Breakfasts

For me, breakfast is the most fun meal of the day. I try to keep it super simple, but there are some mornings that are a little extra, and they need a little kick. The important thing is that you get a healthy start, even when you are running late for a class.

AVOCADO TOAST

VEGETARIAN | SERVES: **2** | PREP TIME: **LESS THAN 5 MINUTES** | COOK TIME: **5 MINUTES**

2 slices sourdough, multigrain, or other bread

1 ripe avocado

Pinch ground black pepper

Juice of ¼ lime

1 teaspoon store-bought pesto

4 cherry tomatoes

Helpful hint: After removing the avocado pit, use the knife to score the flesh and then squeeze it out into the bowl. If you like your avocado on the chunky side, don't worry about mashing it—one less fork to clean!

This recipe is a study in flavor, nutrition, and simplicity. It's as easy as making toast, with just a few added twists that make it so worth the minimal effort. You can toast any bread for this, but sourdough adds a nice bit of flavor that I love. You can make this breakfast even heartier by using multigrain bread.

1. Toast the bread.

2. While the bread toasts, pit the avocado, then scoop the flesh into a bowl and mash it with a fork. Add the pepper and lime juice, then continue to mash until the avocado reaches your desired consistency.

3. Spread each piece of toast with half of the pesto, then top with the mashed avocado.

4. Cut the cherry tomatoes in half and place them on top of the avocado.

Leftover tip: Adding lime juice to the avocado keeps it from turning brown, so you can make one slice of toast now and store the rest of the avocado in an airtight container in the refrigerator for later.

Pesto comes in smaller jars, but if you don't make this recipe often, you might have some left over. Add it to pasta or to guacamole for a nice depth of flavor.

TOASTER OVEN GRANOLA

GLUTEN-FREE, VEGETARIAN | SERVES: **4** | PREP TIME: **LESS THAN 5 MINUTES** | COOK TIME: **4 MINUTES**

1 cup old-fashioned rolled oats (check label for gluten-free)

¼ cup chopped cashews

¼ cup dried cherries

1 tablespoon canola or vegetable oil

3 tablespoons maple syrup

Toaster ovens are so underutilized despite the amazing things they can do. This is a very easy recipe for a sweet and nutritious granola mix you never knew you had to have. Once you know how easy and cheap this granola is, you will make it all the time. It will be your go-to snack to carry to class or your favorite Greek yogurt topping.

1. Preheat your toaster oven to 450°F. Line the toaster oven baking sheet with aluminum foil.

2. In a bowl, mix together the oats, cashews, dried cherries, oil, and syrup.

3. Spread the mixture evenly on the prepared baking sheet and bake for 4 minutes.

Sub in: Real maple syrup isn't cheap, but it sure is tasty. If you can't use the pure stuff, that's okay, too. You can substitute it with a cheaper syrup, especially if you keep some packets handy from your local fast-food spot.

If you don't have the budget for dried cherries, substitute another dried fruit of your choice.

Helpful hint: If you buy oats, cashews, and cherries in the bulk section, you can premeasure to pay for only what you will use, saving money and making prep even easier.

29

VANILLA YOGURT AND BERRY PARFAIT

GLUTEN-FREE OPTION, NO-COOK, VEGETARIAN | SERVES: **1** |
PREP TIME: **LESS THAN 5 MINUTES**

¾ cup vanilla yogurt

¼ cup frozen berries, thawed

2 tablespoons Toaster Oven Granola (page 29) or store-bought granola (check label for gluten-free)

You may not be inclined to eat a parfait, let alone make one. Not everybody is into the idea. But once you try it, you will have to admit it's incredibly tasty and makes you feel great. You can throw together this super-simple, no-cook recipe in a pinch so you can have a good start to your day without a lot of fuss or heavy ingredients.

1. Scoop half of the yogurt into a bowl, mug, or other container.

2. Add the berries and 1 tablespoon of the granola, then top with the remaining yogurt and granola to create a layered look.

Helpful hint: Most individual yogurt cups sold at the store are ¾ cup (6 ounces), so you can just use those as an easy way to get the right amount of yogurt without having to open a larger container and potentially waste the remaining contents.

With some spare dollars: If you have access to and money for fresh strawberries, they can take your parfait to new heights.

EGG WHITE BAGEL SANDWICH

VEGETARIAN | SERVES: **1** | PREP TIME: **LESS THAN 5 MINUTES** | COOK TIME: **LESS THAN 5 MINUTES**

1 tablespoon canola or vegetable oil

1 egg white

1 bagel, sliced

1 slice Cheddar cheese

¼ ripe avocado, sliced

¼ cup baby spinach

1 tomato slice

This hearty, well-rounded breakfast incorporates carbohydrates, vitamins, and protein in one tasty sandwich that is easy to make and a pleasure to eat. It's really cheap to make because it's so produce focused.

1. Heat the oil in a skillet on a hot plate set to medium heat. Add the egg white and cook until it is opaque, about 1 minute. Remove from the heat.

2. Toast the bagel, if desired.

3. Assemble your sandwich with the cheese on the bottom of the bagel, then add the sliced avocado, spinach, sliced tomato, and the fried egg white. Top with the top half of the bagel and enjoy.

Leftover tip: Don't even think about throwing out that leftover produce! You can stretch the ingredients to cover a pack of six bagels, then store the extra sandwiches wrapped in foil or plastic wrap in the refrigerator.

With some spare dollars: Zest up your sandwich with a chipotle sauce or a spicy jalapeño aioli spread on the bottom bagel. Or, for a cheaper way to punch up the flavor, grab some hot sauce packets from your cafeteria.

31

BREAKFAST NACHOS

GLUTEN-FREE | SERVES: **1 TO 2** | PREP TIME: **LESS THAN 5 MINUTES** | COOK TIME: **15 MINUTES**

1 tablespoon canola or vegetable oil

2 eggs, beaten

2 slices turkey bacon

2 cups tortilla chips (check label for gluten-free)

¼ ripe avocado, chopped

¼ cup shredded Cheddar cheese

3 tablespoons jarred salsa

This quick and painless nacho recipe is the best thing to happen to breakfast since burritos. It's the perfect blend of your favorite breakfast components and cheesy, crunchy nacho bliss. This dish can serve another person, but from personal experience, I can tell you these will be gone faster than you think. This inexpensive recipe is a great way to use up leftover ingredients from some of the other recipes in this book.

1. Preheat the toaster oven to 450°F. Line the toaster oven baking sheet with aluminum foil.

2. Heat the oil in a skillet on a hot plate set to medium heat. Add the eggs and cook until they are scrambled, keeping them moving and breaking the curds into small pieces so that they will crumble easily on top of the chips.

3. Place the bacon on the prepared baking sheet. Bake for 7 to 10 minutes or until crispy. Remove from the oven and let cool.

32

4. Place the chips on the tray, then sprinkle the avocado chunks, scrambled egg, and shredded cheese over the chips.

5. Bake for 3 minutes and chop up the bacon.

6. Top the nachos with the bacon and salsa.

Sub in: You can save money and time on this recipe by subbing sliced olives for the bacon. This will reduce the cooking time to less than 5 minutes.

Ingredient tip: The Cheddar cheese doesn't necessarily have to be preshredded. If you have leftover slices from the Egg White Bagel Sandwich (page 31), chop up your desired amount and use that instead.

Leftover tip: Looking for something to do with those unused strips of turkey bacon? Try adding 2 slices to the Cheesy Omelet (page 38). Cook the bacon in the toaster oven just like you did in step 3 for the nachos, then crumble it over the omelet before folding it over with a spatula.

CHERRY, PECAN, AND BROWN SUGAR OATMEAL

VEGETARIAN | SERVES: **1** | PREP TIME: **LESS THAN 5 MINUTES** | COOK TIME: **2 MINUTES**

1 cup
  quick-cooking
  oats

¾ cup milk

¼ teaspoon ground
  cinnamon

Pinch salt

1 tablespoon
  chopped pecans

1 tablespoon
  dried cherries

1 tablespoon
  brown sugar

Sometimes you want a great-tasting, hot breakfast that won't weigh you down or take long to make. Although this isn't an on-the-go meal, you can eat it fast. You just may not want to. The flavors brought together in this nutritious breakfast will make you want to savor every bite. Use the time you save making it to enjoy a few extra minutes of relaxation before you start your day. This breakfast is especially good with cold brew coffee (page 36).

1. In a microwave-safe bowl, combine the oats, milk, cinnamon, and salt. Microwave on high for 2 minutes.

2. Stir and add the pecans, cherries, and brown sugar. Enjoy.

Sub in: You can replace the pecans and cherries with virtually any kind of nut or berry topping. Try using leftover chopped cashews from the Toaster Oven Granola (page 29) and leftover frozen berries from the Vanilla Yogurt and Berry Parfait (page 30). For a completely different take, top the oats with peanut butter and jelly.

Leftover tip: Brown sugar lasts up to 2 years in a pantry, but if any moisture gets in, it can clump and become hard. To prevent spoilage, place a piece of bread in the jar with the brown sugar to keep it dry.

34

BLUEBERRY MUFFIN IN A MUG

VEGETARIAN | SERVES: **1** | PREP TIME: **LESS THAN 5 MINUTES** | COOK TIME: **2 MINUTES**

½ cup all-purpose flour

2 tablespoons brown sugar

½ teaspoon baking powder

½ cup milk

1 tablespoon butter

2 tablespoons blueberries

1 drop vanilla extract

Pinch ground cinnamon

Pinch salt

There is nothing quite like a hot blueberry muffin for breakfast. Although you may not have the luxury of baking delicious, golden-brown muffins in your dorm room, you can create a pretty decent facsimile with a mug and a microwave. Try this once, and you'll be making these muffins all the time.

1. In a bowl, stir together all of the ingredients, then pour the mixture into a microwave-safe mug.

2. Microwave for 2 minutes, then remove the mug from the microwave and let stand for 1 minute. Eat with a spoon or dump the muffin out of the mug to eat by hand.

Sub in: The muffins are just as good when you sub chocolate chips for the blueberries.

Helpful hint: The baking powder is key to keeping the muffin from adhering to the mug in the microwave. You should be able to easily remove the muffin after cooking.

Ingredient tip: You may be wondering what to do with a whole bottle of vanilla extract, but it's actually not as exotic an ingredient as you may think. You can find it in small, 2-ounce bottles in your grocery store's spice section. Use it almost anytime you make something sweet.

35

MAKE YOUR OWN COLD BREW COFFEE

GLUTEN-FREE, NO-COOK, VEGETARIAN | SERVES: **4** |
PREP TIME: **LESS THAN 5 MINUTES, PLUS 12 HOURS TO BREW**

4 cups water

½ cup coarsely ground coffee

Sugar (optional)

Cream or nondairy creamer (optional)

Helpful hint:
To make cold brew, use coarse grinds and refrigerate for at least 12 hours. You can use any vessel and an ordinary coffee filter or cheesecloth to transfer grind-free coffee into a jar or pitcher for storage.

Cold brew is a delicious, smooth, and convenient way to enjoy your coffee that tends to be sweeter and less hard on your stomach than hot coffee. With cold brew waiting in your mini refrigerator, you won't have to mess with a coffee machine in the morning. That means no measuring and no waiting—just pour yourself a cup of rich, dark, caffeinated deliciousness. Even better, because no machine is required, this recipe is very inexpensive.

1. Fill a pitcher with the water and add the coffee grounds. Stir to mix well, let it settle, then stir again until the grounds are dispersed evenly throughout the water.

2. Place the mixture in the refrigerator for a minimum of 12 hours.

3. Remove the mixture from the refrigerator and place a coffee filter inside a quart-size jar. Hold the filter securely over the brim and carefully strain the coffee into the jar.

4. In a drinking glass, add the sugar and cream, if using, then pour in the desired amount of cold brew.

With some spare dollars: Create your own flavored syrup by combining equal parts sugar and your choice of herbal tea.

CHEESY OMELET

GLUTEN-FREE | SERVES: **1** | PREP TIME: **LESS THAN 5 MINUTES** | COOK TIME: **LESS THAN 5 MINUTES**

2 eggs

2 tablespoons milk

1 tablespoon butter

¼ cup shredded cheese (any kind)

Salt

Ground black pepper

With some spare dollars:

Add salsa, veggies, or meats of your choice and make the omelet as thick as you like. You can even incorporate unused ingredients and leftovers into this dish.

Omelets don't have to be intimidating, challenging, or time-consuming. They're as tasty as they are fast and easy to make. Every omelet starts with the same base, but these protein-packed breakfasts can include any combination of toppings you prefer. You can leave this cheesy omelet as is or add whatever frills you prefer. If you have a stash of fast-food condiments, you might add some hot sauce or salsa to this dish.

1. Place a skillet on the hot plate and set the heat to medium.

2. Using a fork, whisk the eggs in a bowl with the milk until smooth.

3. Melt the butter in the skillet, swirl to coat the bottom of the skillet, then pour in the egg mixture. Let the egg mixture cook until the edges are dry, then add the cheese and fold the omelet with a spatula.

4. Slide the omelet out of the skillet onto a plate and add salt and pepper to taste.

Helpful hint: When making an omelet, it's ideal to use a cheese with a low melting temperature. Pepper jack is a great choice because it adds an extra level of flavor. Soft cheeses like Brie and goat cheese are good, too. If Cheddar is all you have, just note that it may not melt completely in the omelet.

FRENCH TOAST IN A MUG

SERVES: **2** | PREP TIME: **LESS THAN 5 MINUTES** | COOK TIME: **45 SECONDS**

2 tablespoons milk

2 eggs

1 teaspoon sugar

1 teaspoon ground cinnamon

1 drop vanilla extract

1 tablespoon butter

2 cups chopped bread

One of my favorite go-to breakfasts is cinnamon-sugar French toast. It can be a little more involved than you usually have time for in college life, but this chunky, pull-apart version you can make in the microwave is a delicious alternative. For best results, use day-old bread. Sourdough is a good choice, but have fun picking your own favorites.

1. In a bowl, mix together the milk, eggs, sugar, cinnamon, and vanilla.

2. Grease the inside of a microwave-safe mug with the butter.

3. Add the bread pieces to the egg mixture and let them soak for a few minutes, until they are completely coated. Transfer the soaked bread to the prepared mug.

4. Microwave on high for 45 seconds.

Helpful hint: Use a fast-food syrup packet for dipping.

39

Pigs in a Blanket
p.44

Snacks, Sides, and Other Tiny Bites

In this chapter, you will find great ideas for fast, inexpensive bites for late-night snacking and on-the-go nutrition. Many of these dishes work well on their own as a quick fix for your hunger, but there are also side dishes that pair nicely with the entrées from chapter 5.

SPICED POPCORN

GLUTEN-FREE, VEGAN | SERVES: **2** | PREP TIME: **5 MINUTES** |
COOK TIME: **2 TO 4 MINUTES**

1 bag plain
   microwaveable
   popcorn, or
   4 cups popped
   popcorn

5 tablespoons
   canola or
   vegetable oil

1¼ teaspoons
   ground cumin

1¼ teaspoons
   chili powder

1¼ teaspoons
   paprika

Pinch cayenne
   pepper

Pinch salt

Pinch ground
   black pepper

There are all kinds of easy ways to make popcorn more inter-esting. My favorite way is this spicy popcorn, which is just a simple spiced coating to give my go-to movie snack a little flavor boost. Making a batch takes very little time, and if stored in an airtight container at room temperature, it can last for a couple of sittings.

1. Microwave the popcorn according to the instructions on the bag. Be sure to stop the microwave when popping slows to 3 seconds apart.

2. While the popcorn is popping, mix the oil, cumin, chili powder, paprika, cayenne pepper, salt, and black pepper in a small dish until blended.

3. Be careful with the hot popcorn bag. Pull the corners at the top of the bag to open and pour the contents into a large mixing bowl.

4. Slowly mix in the seasoning mixture until the popcorn is well-coated.

Sub in: For a sweet mix, try substituting 2 teaspoons of cinnamon sugar and 1 teaspoon of cocoa powder for the cumin, chili powder, and paprika, and omit the cayenne pepper, salt, and black pepper.

42

EASY HOMEMADE DILL PICKLES

GLUTEN-FREE, VEGAN | SERVES: **8** | PREP TIME: **LESS THAN 5 MINUTES, PLUS 2 HOURS TO CHILL** | COOK TIME: **LESS THAN 5 MINUTES**

2 cucumbers

2 garlic cloves, whole

2 sprigs fresh dill

1 cup water

¾ cup white vinegar

1 tablespoon salt

One way to make a meal your own is to add flourishes to your condiments and garnishes. Dill pickles are cheap and easy to make, plus they add a little extra to even the most ordinary sandwich. This recipe is very basic, but once you have it down, you can add new ingredients to give it your own signature flair.

1. On a cutting board, trim off the ends of the cucumbers and cut the cucumbers lengthwise into four long wedges.

2. Place the cucumber wedges in a jar along with the garlic and dill.

3. Set a hot plate to high heat. Pour the water and vinegar into a saucepan, add the salt, and place the pan on the hot plate. Bring the brine to a boil, stir until the salt is completely dissolved, then remove the pan from the heat.

4. Let the hot brine sit for 2 minutes, then pour it into the jar with the cucumbers. Seal and refrigerate for at least 2 hours before serving.

Storage tip:
Keep pickles in a sealed jar in the refrigerator for up to 2 months.

Leftover tip: You can use your leftover dill with canned tuna or salmon. You can also dry it out for shelf storage by hanging it upside down for up to 2 weeks, then crumbling the dry herb into a bowl. Transfer the dill to a jar, and store with other dried herbs and spices.

43

PIGS IN A BLANKET

SERVES: **6** | PREP TIME: **LESS THAN 5 MINUTES** | COOK TIME: **10 MINUTES**

1 (8-ounce) can crescent roll dough

12 cocktail weenies

2 tablespoons butter, at room temperature

Salt

Making your own hors d'oeuvres may seem intimidating, but don't let that stop you from trying this recipe—all this really requires is a little slicing and rolling to yield that perfect savory snack. So, let's grab those ingredients and crank up the toaster oven. This recipe serves six people, but even when you're alone, they have a way of disappearing.

1. Preheat your toaster oven to 375°F. Line the toaster oven baking sheet with aluminum foil.

2. Unroll the dough. There should be 8 rectangles of dough. Lay 4 of them on your work surface and pack up the rest for later (see leftover tip).

3. Cut your 4 dough rectangles into three slender triangles each, then roll a cocktail weenie up inside each one.

4. Brush the rolled-up crescents with the softened butter, using your fingers to spread it evenly around the surface. Sprinkle each roll with salt.

Helpful hint:
Add some flavor by spreading your favorite mustard or cheese on the dough before you roll it up.

5. Place the pigs in a blanket on the prepared baking sheet and bake for 10 minutes or until golden brown.

Leftover tip: Separate the leftover dough between layers of wax paper, then wrap it in foil or plastic. Store it in the refrigerator for a few days, until you're ready to bake the rolls according to the package directions.

SPINACH DIP

GLUTEN-FREE OPTION, VEGETARIAN | SERVES: **2 TO 4** | PREP TIME: **5 MINUTES** | COOK TIME: **2 TO 3 MINUTES**

1 (10-ounce) package frozen spinach

1 (14-ounce) can artichoke hearts, drained and chopped

1 cup shredded mozzarella cheese

1 cup sour cream

½ cup cream cheese, diced

Salt

Ground black pepper

Tortilla chips, for serving (check label for gluten-free)

This is a really great snack if you need to take a study break or if you're hungry but don't necessarily want a full meal. This simple dip takes the pressure off from cooking a full meal if you don't have the time or energy. That way, you can keep up the good habit of cooking and give yourself a little bit of a break, too.

1. Cook the spinach in the microwave according to the package instructions.

2. While the spinach is cooking, combine the chopped artichoke hearts, mozzarella, sour cream, diced cream cheese, and a pinch each of salt and pepper in a microwave-safe mixing bowl. Mix well.

3. Blot the cooked spinach with a paper towel and squeeze out any excess water. Add the drained spinach to the mixing bowl. Mix well.

4. Place the mixing bowl in the microwave and cook on high for 1 minute.

5. Take the bowl out of the microwave, give the mixture a good stir, then return it to the microwave and cook for an additional 90 seconds. Serve with tortilla chips.

45

BRUSCHETTA

VEGETARIAN | MAKES 24 (1/2-INCH-THICK) SLICES | PREP TIME: **LESS THAN 5 MINUTES** | COOK TIME: **2 TO 3 MINUTES**

1 tablespoon
olive oil

1 teaspoon
balsamic vinegar

¼ teaspoon
garlic powder

Salt

Ground black
pepper

1 pint cherry
tomatoes, halved

1 mini baguette

4 fresh basil leaves,
finely chopped

When I am in the zone on a study night, I have the worst time breaking away to eat something. I will starve in place if somebody doesn't literally bring me food, unless I can just grab a snack. So, when I know I'll be hitting the books really hard, I always like to pull up a handy recipe like this bruschetta. I can grab slices and eat them without a second thought. I never have to stop studying, and before I know it, the whole batch is gone! This recipe can serve more than two people (depending on how hungry you are), so it's also an excellent snack or appetizer for when you have company.

1. In a small mixing bowl, combine the oil, vinegar, garlic powder, salt, and pepper. Mix well.

2. Add the cherry tomatoes to the bowl and mix until the tomatoes are well-coated. Set the bowl aside.

3. Cut the baguette into ½- to ¾-inch-thick slices. Make up to 24 slices and set aside any extra bread.

4. Toast the baguette slices in a toaster oven until golden brown.

5. Remove the toasted slices from the toaster oven. Top each with some of the tomato mixture. Finish by sprinkling the bruschetta with the finely chopped basil.

THAI-INSPIRED LETTUCE CUPS

GLUTEN-FREE | SERVES: **2** | PREP TIME: **5 MINUTES** | COOK TIME: **6 TO 10 MINUTES**

2 tablespoons canola or vegetable oil

½ pound ground chicken

¼ cup soy sauce (check label for gluten-free)

½ teaspoon ground ginger

¼ cup chopped peanuts

½ head iceberg lettuce, leaves separated and rinsed

½ cup shredded carrots (optional)

Just because you live in a dorm doesn't mean you can't discover a world of flavors. These Thai-Inspired Lettuce Cups will give you a taste of something that might not be so easy to find on campus. This dish is very simple to prepare and even easier to clean up after. The lettuce cups serve as their own dish, so there's less for you to wash.

1. Pour the oil into a skillet, place the skillet on your hot plate, and set the heat to medium-high. When the oil is hot, add the chicken and cook, stirring to break up the meat, for 5 minutes or until the meat is completely browned (no pink remaining).

2. Add the soy sauce, ground ginger, and chopped peanuts. Stir and cook for 2 minutes.

3. Lay out the lettuce cups on a platter and spoon some of the cooked chicken mixture into each cup. Add the shredded carrots (if using) on top for extra color and texture.

With some spare dollars: Add even more pop to your lettuce cups by incorporating cilantro. Finely chop it and add it to the top of the chicken mixture along with the shredded carrots.

Leftover tip: If you have a leftover half head of lettuce, simply wrap it in plastic and store in the refrigerator until it's time to make a salad or more lettuce cups. You can also sub it in for romaine in other recipes throughout this book.

47

HOMEMADE HUMMUS

GLUTEN-FREE, NO-COOK, VEGAN | SERVES: **2** | PREP TIME: **5 MINUTES**

¼ cup tahini

1 garlic clove

2 tablespoons lemon juice (juice from 1 lemon)

2 tablespoons olive oil

1 (15-ounce) can chickpeas, drained and rinsed

Salt

This hummus recipe is another incredible go-to for convenient snacking. You can take it on the go or make a larger batch for a party with friends. If you can get a food processor, use it, but a blender will do the trick. This recipe calls for tahini, a common ingredient in hummus that's made from sesame seeds. You can also use tahini in a number of Mediterranean dishes, such as baba ghanoush, or, if you really like hummus, you can double or triple this recipe to use up the rest of the jar of tahini.

1. In a blender, combine the tahini, garlic, lemon juice, and olive oil. Pulse until smooth, then add the chickpeas and pulse again until smooth.

2. Add water, 1 tablespoon at a time, pulsing between additions until the hummus reaches your desired consistency. Taste and season with salt.

3. Pour the hummus into a bowl and enjoy with veggies or your choice of bread or pita.

Helpful hint: If you don't have anything to strain your chickpeas with, simply don't open the can all the way. Pour out the liquid while holding the can's lid in place to keep the chickpeas from spilling out. Rinse the chickpeas while they are still in the can, pouring out the water in the same way.

48

CHEESY NACHOS IN A MUG

GLUTEN-FREE, VEGETARIAN | SERVES: **1** | PREP TIME: **LESS THAN 5 MINUTES** | COOK TIME: **1 MINUTE**

1 cup tortilla chips (check label for gluten-free)

3 tablespoons canned refried beans

3 tablespoons jarred salsa

3 tablespoons pickled jalapeño slices

⅓ cup shredded Cheddar cheese

Sour cream (optional)

Easy and fast, this nacho recipe solves the age-old problem: How do you get every chip coated in flavorful toppings? To get the layers just right on a plate takes years of practice, but using a mug is like bowling with bumpers. This stackable nacho recipe takes advantage of the cylindrical property of a coffee mug to keep toppings in place and facilitate layering. It's also the portable nacho solution you never knew you absolutely needed.

1. Place one-third of the tortilla chips in a microwave-safe mug. Add one-third each of the beans, salsa, and jalapeños. Sprinkle 2 tablespoons of the cheese over top.

2. Add another layer of chips, beans, salsa, jalapeños, and 2 tablespoons of cheese.

3. Top with a final layer of chips and the remaining toppings.

4. Microwave on high for 1 minute. Top with a dollop of sour cream, if desired.

Sub in: You can use hot sauce packets or leftover enchilada sauce instead of salsa. If you want less spicy nachos, you can replace the jalapeños with avocado or olives.

Helpful hint: You can also use the canned nacho cheese sauce from the Cheesy Ground Beef Tacos recipe (page 88) if you don't have shredded cheese available.

49

ROSEMARY-GARLIC POTATOES

GLUTEN-FREE, VEGETARIAN | SERVES: **2** | PREP TIME: **LESS THAN 5 MINUTES** | COOK TIME: **15 MINUTES**

1 garlic clove, minced

½ tablespoon butter

¾ pound red or white new potatoes (about 6 potatoes, cut into wedges)

½ tablespoon dried rosemary

Salt

Ground black pepper

The trick to making these potatoes pop is the delicious garlic butter. These potatoes go great with any kind of meat, and they're the perfect dish to bring to a potluck dinner party.

1. In a microwave-safe dish with a lid, combine the garlic and butter. Cover and microwave at 70 percent power for 45 seconds.

2. Remove the dish from the microwave, then add the potatoes, rosemary, salt, and pepper. Mix thoroughly, cover the dish, and microwave on high for 12 to 15 minutes, until the potatoes are tender and easily pierced with a fork.

Helpful hint: To mince garlic, crush the head at the stem with the flat side of the knife to loosen the cloves. Remove a clove and place the widest part of the flat side of the blade down on it. Press on the side of the blade with your palm to loosen the peel. Trim away the root end of the clove and make rough slices, then rotate the knife 90 degrees, and with a rocking motion, make fine slices to mince.

Helpful hint: To crisp up the potatoes after you've microwaved them, place them on a small baking sheet and bake in the toaster oven at 425° for 10-15 minutes.

GARLIC KALE CHIPS

GLUTEN-FREE, VEGAN | SERVES: **1** | PREP TIME: **5 MINUTES** |
COOK TIME: **4 TO 5 MINUTES**

1 bunch kale, stems removed and discarded, leaves cut into chip-size pieces

2 tablespoons olive oil, divided

Salt

When you want to mindlessly chow down on a snack, kale chips are a healthier alternative to popcorn. These crispy greens are a good source of nutrients and very convenient for when you need to bring some food on the go. They are lightweight and satisfying to munch on between classes.

1. Arrange half of the kale pieces on a microwave-safe plate, making sure they are not touching. Drizzle 1 tablespoon of the oil over the kale, season with salt, and microwave until crispy, about 2 to 2½ minutes. Transfer the cooked kale chips to a bowl.

2. Arrange the remaining kale pieces on the plate, drizzle them with the remaining olive oil, and season with salt. Microwave the kale for 2 to 2½ minutes, until crispy.

3. Transfer to the bowl with the rest of the kale chips and enjoy.

51

Caprese Salad
p.54

To-Go Lunches, Solo Dinners, and Late-Night Meals

Welcome to your solution hub for to-go, late-night, and solo meals. If you're like I was in college, you want quick, single-serve meals that don't cost much to make. Fast food is an easy out that ends up costing you hundreds of dollars a month. There is a better way, and it's right here. These small, fast meals are so convenient you won't even have time to think about how much time and money you are saving.

CAPRESE SALAD

GLUTEN-FREE, NO-COOK, VEGETARIAN | SERVES: **1** | PREP TIME: **LESS THAN 5 MINUTES**

10 fresh basil leaves

1 vine-ripened
   tomato, sliced

5 ounces fresh
   mozzarella, sliced

2 tablespoons
   extra-virgin
   olive oil

Salt

Ground black
   pepper

54

With all of its simplicity, this caprese salad is the perfect dish whether you're looking for a late-night meal or packing something to go. This salad bursts with bright, juicy tomato, peppery basil, and thick, soft mozzarella. It's light and satisfying at the same time, which makes it ideal for any occasion. This recipe calls for fresh basil because it is an essential ingredient for both flavor and composition, so don't substitute dry basil for fresh as you might do with other recipes.

1. Place a basil leaf on top of a slice of tomato. Add a slice of mozzarella and another basil leaf, then start again with another tomato slice, alternating with mozzarella and using basil in between each layer.

2. When the stack is complete, drizzle it with olive oil and season to taste with salt and pepper.

Helpful hint: If you can't get your hands on a vine-ripened tomato, a regular tomato will do. However, it's worth noting that vine-ripened tomatoes tend to be more flavorful and add depth to your overall dish, whereas alternatives tend to be more watery.

Leftover tip: Save a couple of mozzarella slices and a slice of tomato for making a Mozzarella Sandwich (page 60) for lunch the next day.

STRAWBERRY-PECAN SALAD

GLUTEN-FREE, NO-COOK, VEGAN | SERVES: 1 | PREP TIME: LESS THAN 5 MINUTES

FOR THE DRESSING

¼ cup extra-virgin olive oil

1 teaspoon lemon juice

½ teaspoon Dijon mustard

Salt

Ground black pepper

FOR THE SALAD

½ cup chopped romaine lettuce

4 strawberries, halved

2 tablespoons blueberries

2 tablespoons halved pecans

This bright berry and pecan mix gives your brain everything you need as you head into an all-nighter or take a midday break to clear your head and regain focus. There are two parts to this recipe: an easy-to-make delicious salad and a phenomenal dressing that you can use on your other favorite salads.

TO MAKE THE DRESSING

Combine the olive oil, lemon juice, Dijon mustard, salt, and pepper in a small bowl. Mix well to create an even mixture.

TO MAKE THE SALAD

1. In a medium bowl, toss together the romaine, strawberries, blueberries, and pecans.

2. Drizzle your desired amount of dressing over the salad and toss again before serving.

Helpful hint: If the dressing is too tart, you can neutralize the tartness by adding ½ teaspoon of sugar to the mixture.

THAI-INSPIRED CHICKEN SALAD

FOR THE PEANUT SAUCE

5 tablespoons peanut butter

2 tablespoons soy sauce

1 tablespoon rice wine vinegar

1 tablespoon brown sugar

½ tablespoon garlic powder

This salad is a perfectly balanced meal packed with bright flavors and savory goodness. The only thing you have to cook is the chicken, and as a bonus, you learn how to make an amazing peanut sauce that's also great as a dipping sauce or a super-easy sauce for noodles. You can make as much sauce as you like, and store leftovers in an airtight container in the refrigerator for as long as two weeks.

TO MAKE THE PEANUT SAUCE

In a medium bowl, mix together the peanut butter, soy sauce, vinegar, brown sugar, and garlic powder.

TO MAKE THE SALAD

1. Pour the oil into a skillet, set the skillet on a hot plate, and set the hot plate to medium heat.

1 tablespoon
   canola or
   vegetable oil
1 boneless, skinless
   chicken thigh
2 tablespoons
   teriyaki sauce
½ cup chopped
   romaine lettuce
2 tablespoons
   shredded carrots
2 tablespoons
   canned mandarin
   oranges
1 teaspoon
   chopped fresh
   cilantro

2. Put the chicken in a bowl, add the teriyaki sauce, and turn to coat the chicken thoroughly.

3. Add the chicken to the hot skillet and cook for 2 minutes, then flip and cook for 3 minutes or until cooked through. Use a meat thermometer to make sure the chicken's internal temperature is 165°F.

4. Remove the skillet from the heat and transfer the chicken to a cutting board. Cut the chicken into ½-inch chunks.

5. In a large bowl, toss together the romaine, carrots, oranges, cilantro, and peanut sauce. Top the salad with the chicken before serving.

Leftover tip: Chicken thighs are more affordable than chicken breasts, but you can use leftover meat from a store-bought rotisserie chicken or the Slow-Cooker Whole Chicken recipe in chapter 5 of this book (page 84). You can make several recipes in this book using leftovers from a precooked chicken.

TUNA SALAD SANDWICH

1 (5-ounce) can tuna fish, drained

2 tablespoons mayonnaise

½ cup chopped celery

Salt

Ground black pepper

2 slices sourdough or other bread

When you want a delicious, protein-packed, on-the-go meal, a tuna fish sandwich is one of the best options. It's one of the easiest things you can make, and it doesn't require any cooking. Always keep a couple of cans of tuna in your makeshift pantry so that you can whip up a healthy meal at a moment's notice.

1. In a bowl, combine the tuna, mayonnaise, celery, and salt and pepper to taste until all ingredients are equally incorporated.

2. Spoon the tuna mixture onto a slice of bread and spread it out evenly.

3. Top with the second slice of bread. Cut in half and enjoy.

Helpful hint: If you have a toaster oven, you can toast the bread first for a nice crunch to counter the softness of the tuna. You can even toast the bread with the tuna on top of it. Spread the tuna on the bread, then toast the tuna-topped bread with the top slice of bread beside it.

You can brighten up the flavor by squeezing some fresh lemon juice into the tuna mixture.

58

VEGETABLE WRAP

NO-COOK, VEGAN | SERVES: **1** | PREP TIME: **LESS THAN 5 MINUTES**

3 tablespoons
  Homemade
  Hummus
  (page 48)

1 large whole wheat
  or flour tortilla

½ cucumber,
  cut into long,
  thin spears

¼ cup chopped
  romaine lettuce

2 tablespoons
  shredded carrots

One easy way to have a light and healthy snack in no time is to wrap up some veggies with hummus. It's a great use for leftover veggies and hummus—just switch it up depending on what you have hanging out in the refrigerator.

1. Spread the hummus evenly over the tortilla. Arrange the cucumber spears in columns across half of the tortilla, then add the romaine and shredded carrots.

2. Roll the tortilla from the toppings side to the other side to create a wrap. Slice in half and enjoy.

With some spare dollars: Add a balsamic vinaigrette or your favorite salad dressing. Just drizzle it over the veggies before you roll up the tortilla.

59

MOZZARELLA SANDWICH

VEGETARIAN | SERVES: **1** | PREP TIME: **5 MINUTES**

1 tablespoon store-bought pesto

2 slices sourdough or other bread, toasted if desired

1 tomato slice

2 ounces fresh mozzarella, sliced

Salt

Ground black pepper

Mozzarella is often just the trick you need to curb hunger and regain focus during your day. If you find that your hunger is getting the better of you and you don't have time to make a full-blown meal, mozzarella can give you the substance you need in the simplest of packages. Although this recipe calls for a very specific list of ingredients, you likely already have them, and there are additional possibilities depending on what other leftovers you have.

1. Spread the pesto on one slice of bread. Add the tomato and sliced mozzarella, then sprinkle on salt and pepper to taste.

2. Complete the sandwich by adding the top piece of bread. Slice the sandwich in half and enjoy.

Helpful hint: You can use any leftover veggies you have in the refrigerator for this sandwich. It's an excellent way to use up grocery items so that you don't have to throw them out or buy more food.

EASY QUESADILLA

VEGETARIAN | SERVES: **1** | PREP TIME: **5 MINUTES** | COOK TIME: **5 MINUTES**

1 teaspoon canola or vegetable oil

1 large tortilla

1/3 cup shredded Cheddar cheese

2 tablespoons canned black beans

2 tablespoons pickled jalapeños

2 tablespoons finely diced red bell pepper

A good quesadilla with a crispy grilled tortilla and gooey center is not hard to make. You can make one in less than 10 minutes with a hot plate and a skillet. This quesadilla is very flavorful, with a little bit of spice and a nice dose of plant-based protein. However, you can totally bulk it up with rice or any leftover meats you've been saving.

1. Pour the oil into a skillet, place the skillet on a hot plate, and set the hot plate to medium heat.

2. Place the tortilla in the hot skillet, then add the cheese, beans, jalapeños, and bell pepper to one half of the tortilla. With a spatula, fold over the tortilla to cover the cheese, beans, and peppers. Press down firmly with the spatula to let the melting cheese adhere to the top of the tortilla. Hold for 1 minute.

3. After cooking for 3 minutes, use the spatula to flip the quesadilla, then let it cook for 2 more minutes.

4. Slide the quesadilla onto a cutting board. Cut it into thirds or quarters and enjoy.

Helpful hint: Make sure you buy tortillas that will fit in your skillet. If the tortilla won't fit or you are in a big hurry, you can prepare this snack in the microwave. Heat on a microwave-safe plate for 45 seconds, flip, and cook for another 15 seconds.

61

PEANUT BUTTER AND BANANA WRAP

NO-COOK, VEGETARIAN | SERVES: **1** | PREP TIME: **5 MINUTES**

2 tablespoons creamy peanut butter

1 flour tortilla

1 tablespoon honey

2 tablespoons chocolate chips

1 banana, peeled and sliced lengthwise

Enjoy this peanut butter and jelly alternative for a quick break-fast, lunch, or snack. Not only is it a great way to use up leftover flour tortillas, it's also a nutrient-packed meal that tastes like an indulgence. Plus, it's one of the few meals that doesn't result in any dirty dishes.

1. Spread the peanut butter across the surface of the tortilla. Drizzle the tortilla with honey and scatter the chocolate chips evenly. Pile the banana slices on one side of the tortilla, from top to bottom.

2. Beginning with the banana side, tightly roll the tortilla all the way across.

62

BBQ CHICKEN
FRENCH BREAD PIZZA

SERVES: 8 | PREP TIME: 5 MINUTES | COOK TIME: 5 MINUTES

1 loaf French bread

2 teaspoons extra-virgin olive oil

¼ cup barbecue sauce

½ cup shredded Cheddar cheese

½ cup shredded low-moisture mozzarella cheese

¼ red onion, chopped

½ cup diced Slow-Cooker Whole Chicken (page 84) or store-bought rotisserie chicken

1 tablespoon chopped fresh cilantro

This French bread pizza recipe is so easy to make, delivering gourmet pizza flavor even on a tight budget. Plan to make it when you have extra cooked chicken in your fridge—either homemade or store-bought—and, once you learn the basic method, explore different pizza topping ideas.

1. Preheat the toaster oven to 350°F.

2. Quarter the loaf of French bread by cutting it lengthwise and then again across the center so that two pieces can fit side by side in your toaster oven. Brush olive oil on top of the bread.

3. Spread the barbecue sauce across the top of the bread, then sprinkle on the Cheddar cheese, mozzarella cheese, onion, and chicken.

4. Bake for 5 minutes or until the cheese has melted. Garnish with cilantro.

Leftover tip: Red onion and cilantro make a great pair in a number of dishes. Use them in a salad or in a corn salsa.

PESTO PASTA IN A MUG

VEGETARIAN | SERVES: **1** | PREP TIME: **LESS THAN 5 MINUTES** | COOK TIME: **10 TO 15 MINUTES**

¾ cup dried elbow macaroni

2 tablespoons store-bought pesto

1 tablespoon grated Parmesan cheese

Ground black pepper

If you have pesto in your refrigerator, this microwave pasta dish is a great way to get some extra mileage out of it. You can also use any other sauce you have on hand or a different type of pasta. However, there is nothing quite like the taste of pesto, Parmesan, and pepper in perfect harmony.

1. Pour the pasta into a microwave-safe mug and cover with water. Microwave for 3 minutes longer than the stovetop instructions indicate on the box of pasta.

2. Drain the water out of the mug and stir in the pesto and parmesan. Add pepper to taste. Eat with a spoon directly out of the mug.

Leftover tip: Use any Parmesan cheese you have left over to top off the Pizza in a Mug (page 78).

INSTANT MAC 'N' CHEESE

VEGETARIAN | SERVES: **1** | PREP TIME: **LESS THAN 5 MINUTES** |
COOK TIME: **LESS THAN 5 MINUTES**

⅓ cup dried pasta

½ cup water

¼ cup grated Parmesan cheese

¼ cup 2 percent milk

½ cup shredded Cheddar cheese

This is a super fast way to make great-tasting macaroni and cheese in the microwave, and the portion size is way more satisfying than the single cups of the instant stuff they sell at the store. In five minutes, you can have creamy macaroni and cheese like never before. The two-cheese blend of Cheddar and Parmesan creates an addictive balance that will keep you digging in for every last noodle.

1. In a microwave-safe bowl or large mug, combine the pasta and water. Stir with a fork and microwave for 90 seconds. Don't worry about the overflow.

2. Stir again with a fork and microwave for an additional 2 minutes, until all of the water has evaporated or been absorbed.

3. Stir in the Parmesan, milk, and Cheddar and microwave for 1 minute. Stir with a fork before eating.

Helpful hint: Include a dash of pepper with the cheese for some additional zip.

65

TURKEY, SPINACH, AND ARTICHOKE SANDWICH

NO-COOK | SERVES: 1 | PREP TIME: 5 MINUTES

2 teaspoons
  yellow mustard

2 slices bread

4 to 8 slices
  deli turkey

6 fresh spinach
  leaves

2 canned artichoke
  hearts, sliced

1 slice Cheddar
  cheese

There's a reason sandwiches often taste better at delis and restaurants than they do at home: They have more meat! With that in mind, the number of turkey slices is just a suggestion—go big if you can.

1. Spread the mustard on one of the bread slices. Fold the turkey slices and place them on top of the bread. Be sure to cover the whole slice of bread with the turkey. Make this layer of the sandwich as thick as you like.

2. Add the spinach, artichoke, and cheese on top of the turkey.

3. Top the sandwich with the other slice of bread and cut down the center.

Helpful hint: When you buy turkey meat at the deli, you determine how much you get and how thick the turkey is sliced. Not only do you get a customized sandwich, you prevent waste and save money by only purchasing what you need. For a heartier sandwich, I recommend buying ¼ pound of thinly sliced turkey.

Leftover tip: Artichoke hearts can be used to add big flavor to many different dishes. Try chopping some up and adding them to a bowl of plain ramen with shredded Parmesan cheese.

QUINOA FRUIT SALAD

VEGAN | SERVES: 1 | PREP TIME: 5 MINUTES | COOK TIME: 10 MINUTES

½ cup uncooked quinoa, rinsed

¾ cup water

1 tablespoon finely chopped fresh mint

½ cup berries or other chopped fresh fruit

Extra-virgin olive oil

Salt

Ground black pepper

There are three main components to this incredibly simple bowl meal that make it so nice to have as part of your go-to routine. The quinoa is exceptionally high in fiber and rich in protein. Berries are rich in antioxidants and a host of other nutrients that offer potential health benefits like lower cholesterol. Mint is especially good for digestion and is even thought to improve brain function. All of these healthy components together make a tasty meal that you can enjoy anywhere at any time.

1. Combine the quinoa and water in a microwave-safe bowl. Microwave on high, uncovered, for 6 minutes. Then, reduce the power level to 80 percent and cook for another 2 minutes.

2. Meanwhile, mix the mint and berries in a separate bowl and drizzle with the olive oil. Toss until the whole fruit salad is lightly coated in oil.

3. Drain the water from the quinoa and combine it with the fruit mixture. Add salt and pepper to taste.

67

CHICKEN SALAD WRAP

NO-COOK | SERVES: 1 | PREP TIME: **5 MINUTES**

½ cup diced Slow-Cooker Whole Chicken (page 84) or store-bought rotisserie chicken

1 celery stalk, chopped

1 tablespoon slivered almonds

⅓ cup mayonnaise

1 white or whole wheat flour tortilla

⅓ cup chopped romaine lettuce

Salt

Ground black pepper

This recipe is great for using up tortillas, and it's a handy way to use chicken salad. This chicken salad is slightly different from the Tuna Salad Sandwich (page 58), but feel free to interchange them. The almonds in this recipe add an unexpected boost of protein and fiber to help you meet the demands of a busy day.

1. In a mixing bowl, combine the cooked chicken, celery, almonds, and mayonnaise. Stir well.

2. Scoop the chicken mixture onto the lower half of the tortilla. Add the romaine lettuce on top of the chicken and sprinkle with salt and pepper to taste.

3. Fold in both sides of the tortilla to close the ends, then roll tightly from the bottom up.

Leftover tip: Almonds also go great with yogurt! Throw any extras you have into the Vanilla Yogurt and Berry Parfait (30) if you don't feel like making or buying granola.

MICROWAVE "FRIED" RICE

VEGETARIAN | SERVES: **1** | PREP TIME: **LESS THAN 5 MINUTES** | COOK TIME: **10 MINUTES**

1⅓ cups water

1 teaspoon sesame oil

1 tablespoon soy sauce

½ cup uncooked white rice

½ cup frozen stir-fry vegetables

2 eggs

Salt

Ground black pepper

¼ teaspoon onion powder

Fried rice is more than a side dish. It has everything that a balanced meal needs—grains, vegetables, and protein—all in one convenient and tasty bowl. The main obstacle in making fried rice is how difficult it is to get all these elements to work together. It's a lot even for cooks with a proper kitchen. Before you run out to buy an electric wok, try this microwave version that will change everything.

1. In a microwave-safe bowl or casserole dish with a lid, mix together the water, sesame oil, and soy sauce. Stir in the rice, cover the bowl, and microwave on high for 6 to 8 minutes or until the rice is fluffy.

2. Remove the bowl from the microwave and add the frozen vegetables. Set aside.

3. Crack the eggs into a microwave-safe mug and beat them with a spoon or fork. Microwave on high for 90 seconds.

4. Clean the spoon and use it to break up the eggs inside the mug. They should look scrambled.

5. Mix the scrambled egg into the rice and season with salt, pepper, and the onion powder.

6. Cover the bowl and microwave on high for an additional 45 seconds.

69

UPGRADED RAMEN

2½ cups water

Salt

1 egg, at room temperature

1 package instant ramen, any flavor

2 tablespoons finely diced red bell pepper

2 tablespoons shredded carrots

2 tablespoons finely chopped broccoli

For this upgrade to your typical ramen noodle soup, all you need is a microwave and a hot plate. This recipe even includes directions for soft-boiling an egg in the microwave.

1. To soft-boil the egg, pour the water into a microwave-safe bowl or casserole dish with a lid and add a pinch or two of salt. Microwave uncovered for 90 seconds or until the water begins to boil. Gently drop the egg into the hot water and cover the bowl with the lid. Microwave for 1 minute and 45 seconds.

2. While the egg cooks, fill a bowl with ice water. When the timer stops, use tongs to gently remove the egg from the hot water and transfer it to the ice water to stop the cooking process.

3. In a saucepan on a hot plate, cook the ramen with the included seasoning pouch as instructed on the package.

4. Place the bell pepper, carrots, and broccoli in a heatproof bowl. When the ramen is done, pour the noodles and broth over the vegetables and stir well.

5. To finish the dish, peel the egg, cut it in half, and place it on top of the soup.

70

JAZZING UP RAMEN

You can perk up instant ramen and give it a fresh take by adding a simple ingredient:

- **Egg:** Stir the seasoning mix into the ramen, take the noodles off the heat, crack an egg into the bowl, and cover for one minute for a poached effect. You could also top the ramen with a halved soft-boiled egg.
- **Coconut milk:** Add this to fancy up your ramen broth.
- **Peanut butter:** This is a naturally creamy and flavorful way to add complexity to your ramen.
- **American cheese:** Add a slice or two to add a silky texture to your broth.

PARMESAN-GARLIC ALFREDO

VEGETARIAN | SERVES: **1** | PREP TIME: **LESS THAN 5 MINUTES** | COOK TIME: **5 MINUTES**

1 package instant ramen, seasoning packet discarded or reserved for another use

2 tablespoons store-bought Alfredo sauce

1 teaspoon butter

¼ teaspoon garlic powder

Salt

Ground black pepper

2 tablespoons finely chopped mushrooms

1 tablespoon grated Parmesan cheese

There is a good reason why ramen is known as a staple for college students. You can't get much cheaper or simpler than hot water added to a cup of 30-cent noodles. The noodles themselves are full of untapped potential. Pasta is fairly inexpensive, but you can stretch your dollars even more by using ramen noodles in place of traditional Italian pasta. This garlic Alfredo spin is a fresh take on that old dorm-room standby.

1. Break up the ramen square, place it in a microwave-safe mug, and pour in just enough water to cover the noodles. Microwave the noodles according to the instructions on the packet, but do not use the seasoning. Drain the excess liquid.

2. Add the Alfredo sauce, butter, garlic powder, and salt and pepper to taste to the mug. Mix well.

3. Microwave for 30 seconds to melt the butter, stir the noodles, then add the mushrooms and microwave for 15 more seconds. Top with Parmesan cheese, and enjoy.

Leftover tip: An opened jar of Alfredo sauce is good for 2 weeks when refrigerated or 3 months when frozen. Use leftover Alfredo as an easy sauce the next time you make pasta.

THAI-INSPIRED CHICKEN NOODLE BOWL

SERVES: **1** | PREP TIME: **5 MINUTES** | COOK TIME: **5 MINUTES**

1 package instant ramen, seasoning packet discarded or reserved for another use

⅓ cup frozen stir-fry vegetables

2 tablespoons chopped canned water chestnuts

2 tablespoons finely diced Slow-Cooker Whole Chicken (page 84) or store-bought rotisserie chicken

Red pepper flakes

Salt

Ground black pepper

¼ cup Peanut Sauce (page 56)

This delicious ramen-based recipe is amazingly cheap and flavorful. Stir-fry vegetables are nice to have on hand if you have a freezer because you can use them in multiple single-serve meals. This recipe also uses the peanut sauce we used in the Thai-Inspired Chicken Salad (page 56). Since it uses leftovers, this recipe is especially convenient. My favorite component to this recipe is the water chestnuts, which are not a common ingredient, but you will find that having these available is also very handy.

1. Microwave the ramen noodles according to the instructions on the packet, but do not use the seasoning. Drain the excess liquid.

2. Once the ramen is cooked, put the stir-fry veggies in a microwave-safe mug and cover with water. Microwave for 45 seconds, then drain.

3. Add the veggies, water chestnuts, and cooked chicken to the ramen; season with red pepper, salt, and black pepper to taste; and stir well.

4. Top with the peanut sauce and stir once more before eating.

Helpful hint: If you don't have the frozen storage space for stir-fry vegetables, you can make a bigger batch of this meal and store it in individual containers in your refrigerator to save time on future meals.

73

VEGETARIAN BURRITO BOWL

⅓ cup uncooked white rice

½ cup water

2 tablespoons canned black beans

2 tablespoons shredded Cheddar cheese

2 tablespoons canned diced tomatoes

1 tablespoon jarred salsa

1 tablespoon sour cream

1 lime slice

1 teaspoon chopped fresh cilantro

The best recipes to make at home are the ones you typically pay a bundle for in the outside world. Fast-casual restaurants are deceptively high priced, especially if you make a habit of going to these places several times per week. They also routinely change the portions and the pricing to provide less of a value year after year. With your own burrito bowl recipe, you can satisfy that craving for a fraction of the cost, and you always know exactly how much food you have. This is a pretty standard burrito bowl, and it's vegetarian. Of course, you could add meat to this entrée.

1. Pour the rice and water into a microwave-safe bowl and cover with a lid. Microwave on high for 5 minutes.

2. Check that the rice is cooked before proceeding. If it's not cooked, cook for another minute. Continue checking and cooking until the rice is fluffy.

3. Add the beans, Cheddar, tomatoes, salsa, and sour cream to the rice. Squeeze lime juice over the entire bowl and sprinkle with the cilantro.

With some extra dollars: If you are not vegetarian, you can add a meat of your choice to bulk up the meal. Shredded Slow-Cooker Whole Chicken (page 84) or store-bought rotisserie chicken would work well. Tortilla chips make a great add-in or an alternative to silverware—use them instead of a fork to scoop up each bite.

Leftover tip: You can make several of these burrito bowls without buying more ingredients if you keep cans and jars properly refrigerated in sealed containers. Have these ingredients handy for a week of easy meals.

EASY COCONUT CURRY

VEGAN | SERVES: **1** | PREP TIME: **5 MINUTES** | COOK TIME: **10 MINUTES**

½ cup uncooked
white rice

½ cup water

½ teaspoon yellow
curry powder

⅓ cup canned
coconut milk

2 tablespoons
finely diced red
bell pepper

1 teaspoon
chopped fresh
cilantro

1 lime wedge

Salt

Not all fast, easy recipes have to be something you can leave with in a hurry or eat while you're walking. This is a great, cheap meal that's full of flavor. Rice is one of the most budget-friendly ingredients, and it has a long shelf life, so anything you can do with rice is a tremendous help. This curry recipe gives more dimension to the possibilities of rice, and it's pretty easy to make.

1. Pour the rice and water into a microwave-safe bowl and cover with a lid. Microwave on high for 5 minutes. Check that the rice is cooked. If it's not cooked, cook for another minute. Continue checking and cooking until the rice is fluffy.

2. In a separate bowl, whisk together the curry powder and coconut milk, then stir in the bell pepper and cilantro.

3. When the rice is cooked, pour the curry over the top of the rice and squeeze in the lime juice. Season with salt, stir well, and enjoy.

MICROWAVE RISOTTO

GLUTEN-FREE | SERVES: 1 | PREP TIME: 5 MINUTES | COOK TIME: 25 MINUTES

1 teaspoon butter

1 teaspoon extra-virgin olive oil

1/4 cup uncooked arborio rice

2/3 cup chicken broth

1 teaspoon grated Parmesan cheese

Salt

Ground black pepper

Risotto is creamy and delightful. It's packed with flavor, and with this recipe, it is so easy to make. This is an unusual recipe because even though the steps are simple and the ingredients list is short, it takes a little bit of time. But microwave risotto is well worth the wait. Once you have this recipe down, you can experiment with additional flavors.

1. Put the butter and oil in a microwave-safe bowl and cook uncovered for 2 minutes on high.

2. Carefully remove the bowl from the microwave, stir in the rice, and microwave for 4 minutes on high. Pour in the broth and microwave for another 9 minutes. Stir the rice and micro-wave for another 9 minutes.

3. When the risotto is done cooking, fold in the Parmesan cheese, season with salt and pepper, and enjoy.

With some spare dollars: You can add more flavors by incorporating other seasonings such as garlic powder. Just 1/4 teaspoon can change the whole dish.

77

PIZZA IN A MUG

VEGETARIAN | SERVES: **1** | PREP TIME: **5 MINUTES** | COOK TIME: **70 SECONDS**

4 tablespoons all-purpose flour

⅛ teaspoon baking powder

Pinch baking soda

Pinch salt

3 tablespoons milk

1 tablespoon extra-virgin olive oil

1 tablespoon store-bought pizza sauce or marinara sauce

1 tablespoon shredded low-moisture mozzarella cheese

In this recipe, you quickly make the dough and add all the ingredients to it in your mug. It's a great quick fix of microwave pizza bliss. This pizza is ideal for a late-night meal, but it also makes a mean breakfast.

1. In a microwave-safe mug, mix together the flour, baking powder, baking soda, and salt. Stir in the milk and oil to create a dough.

2. Spread the dough out evenly, then spoon the pizza sauce on top, followed by the cheese and any other desired toppings.

3. Microwave on high for 70 seconds.

CHEESY BROCCOLI
AND RICE CASSEROLE

GLUTEN-FREE, VEGETARIAN | SERVES: **1** | PREP TIME: **5 MINUTES** | COOK TIME: **7 MINUTES**

⅓ cup uncooked white rice

½ cup water

⅓ cup frozen broccoli florets

⅓ cup shredded Cheddar cheese

Pinch garlic powder

Salt

Ground black pepper

Casseroles are amazing, but they aren't usually thought of as typical dorm room fare. If you can make and store an entire casserole, more power to you, but if your space is limited, that doesn't mean you need to be left out of the fun. One of the advantages of casseroles is how complete they are on their own. You don't need any sides to make a balanced meal. Once you get past the challenge of reducing the batch, you can enjoy your own personal-size casserole anytime you want. Because we make this casserole in the microwave, it's also super fast.

1. Pour the rice and water into a microwave-safe bowl or casserole dish with a lid. Cover and microwave on high for 5 minutes.

2. In another microwave-safe bowl, microwave the broccoli for 45 seconds.

3. Drain the water from the cooked rice and stir in the broccoli. Add the cheese, garlic powder, and salt and pepper to taste.

4. Microwave uncovered for another 45 seconds.

With some spare dollars: You can bulk up this casserole with a protein, like Slow-Cooker Whole Chicken (page 84) or some leftover meat you have in the refrigerator.

CHICKEN AND AVOCADO PITA SANDWICH

NO-COOK | SERVES: **1** | PREP TIME: **5 MINUTES**

3 tablespoons finely chopped Slow-Cooker Whole Chicken (page 84) or store-bought rotisserie chicken

Pinch garlic powder

1 tablespoon chopped fresh cilantro

1 slice Swiss cheese

1 pita pocket

½ ripe avocado, pitted and sliced

3 tablespoons halved cherry tomatoes

1 lime wedge

This nutritious pita sandwich is simple to make and requires no cooking. Plus, it's easy to take with you if you are in a hurry to get to work or class. If you don't feel like making slow-cooker chicken or buying a rotisserie chicken, you can also buy super-cheap cooked chicken in a can.

1. In a mixing bowl, toss the chicken with the garlic powder and cilantro.

2. Place the cheese in the pita pocket, then add the seasoned chicken, sliced avocado, and tomatoes. Garnish with lime juice.

Storage tip: After preserving the remaining avocado half with lime, wrap it in plastic or keep it in an airtight container in the refrigerator for another recipe.

With some spare dollars: Dress up your pita with mustard, mayonnaise, or your favorite salad dressing.

BUFFALO CHICKEN PINWHEELS

NO-COOK | SERVES: 1 | PREP TIME: 5 MINUTES

¼ cup diced
   Slow-Cooker
   Whole Chicken
   (page 84) or
   store-bought
   rotisserie chicken

1 tablespoon
   buffalo sauce

3 tablespoons
   cream cheese

1 large flour tortilla

3 tablespoons
   shredded
   Cheddar cheese

These pinwheels make an excellent quick meal with lots of protein. I love the hotness of the wing sauce on the chicken coupled with the cooling effect of the cream cheese. It's one of my favorite combinations, and you can use it when preparing other meals as well.

1. In a mixing bowl, toss the chicken with the buffalo sauce.

2. Using a spoon, spread the cream cheese over the whole surface of the tortilla. Scatter the Cheddar cheese and diced chicken over the tortilla and roll it up tightly.

3. Trim and discard the ends of the tortilla roll, then slice the roll into 2-inch-thick pinwheels.

With some spare dollars: Add finely chopped celery or substitute some crumbled blue cheese for the shredded Cheddar cheese to add some texture and additional flare.

Sub in: To make this a hot meal, place the pinwheels on a small baking sheet, and bake in the toaster oven at 375°F for 3 to 5 minutes.

Leftover tip: Make a delicious dipping sauce with leftover buffalo sauce by mixing in 4 tablespoons of ranch for every tablespoon of buffalo sauce.

81

**Slow-Cooker Spaghetti
Marinara p.101**

5

Big Eats for Friends, Lovers, and Your Weird Roommate

Don't be surprised by the recipes for these larger meals. The ingredient lists are a bit longer, but they are so cost-effective you won't believe it. Plus, they're simple to make, and you'll really appreciate how much more you get out of these meals as leftovers or sharable entrées. Maximize your modest cooking quarters by utilizing all of your essentials to the fullest.

SLOW-COOKER WHOLE CHICKEN

GLUTEN-FREE | SERVES: **8** | PREP TIME: **5 MINUTES** | COOK TIME: **5 HOURS**

1 white onion, chopped

2 teaspoons salt

2 teaspoons paprika

½ teaspoon cayenne pepper

1 teaspoon chopped fresh thyme

1½ teaspoons ground black pepper

1 teaspoon onion powder

½ teaspoon garlic powder

1 whole chicken, gizzard removed and discarded

This handy recipe highlights an amazing rub that you can use on anything, but what I really love is that it makes enough meat for lunches and dinners throughout the week. As you may have noticed, there are quite a few recipes that call for cooked chicken throughout this book—the Chicken Salad Wrap (page 68), Buffalo Chicken Pinwheels (page 81), and more—so if you have access to a slow cooker, you'll get a lot of use out of this recipe. Unless you are serving it at a dinner party, once the chicken is done cooking, carve it, pull all the meat from the bones, and store the meat in separate airtight containers in your refrigerator for up to four days.

1. Place the chopped onion in a slow cooker.

2. In a bowl, mix together the salt, paprika, cayenne pepper, thyme, black pepper, onion powder, and garlic powder. Rub this mixture all over the chicken, making sure to spread it evenly.

3. Place the chicken on top of the onion in the slow cooker, then wash your hands thoroughly with soap and warm water.

4. Cook on high for 4 to 5 hours or until the chicken's internal temperature reaches 165°F.

Sub in: If you don't have a slow cooker to make this recipe, you can buy a cooked rotisserie chicken from the store to use in any of the recipes that call for cooked chicken.

LEMON-PEPPER CHICKEN

GLUTEN-FREE | SERVES **3** | PREP TIME **5 MINUTES** | COOK TIME **20 MINUTES**

3 boneless, skinless chicken thighs, cut in half

3 tablespoons extra-virgin olive oil

1 lemon, cut into 6 wedges

¼ teaspoon ground black pepper

Pinch salt

The flavors of lemon and black pepper perk up chicken and give it some terrific zest, making it seem elevated, even though this recipe couldn't be simpler. To make it a meal, pair the chicken with a side of microwaved vegetables or instant mashed potatoes, or serve it over rice or buttered pasta with garlic.

1. Preheat the oven or toaster oven to 400°F. Line a baking sheet with aluminum foil.

2. Place the chicken pieces on the prepared baking sheet and brush them all over with the olive oil. Squeeze 1 lemon wedge over each piece of chicken, then place the squeezed lemon on top of the chicken piece. Sprinkle the pepper over the chicken pieces and season them with a pinch of salt.

3. Bake for 20 minutes or until the chicken's internal temperature reaches 165°F. Remove from the oven and enjoy.

Helpful hint: Whenever you work with raw chicken, be sure to wash your hands thoroughly with soap and warm water before touching anything else.

85

SHREDDED CHICKEN
STREET TACOS 🔲

GLUTEN-FREE | SERVES: **2** | PREP TIME: **5 MINUTES** | COOK TIME: **45 SECONDS**

1 cup shredded Slow-Cooker Whole Chicken (page 84) or store-bought rotisserie chicken

½ cup store-bought salsa (not pico de gallo)

6 corn tortillas

¼ cup sour cream

¼ cup shredded Cheddar cheese or Mexican-cheese blend

2 tablespoons finely chopped scallions or white onion (optional)

2 lime wedges (optional)

This is such an exciting recipe, because it's simple to make. It really only requires some basic assembly. Using cooked chicken means you can save time and use up leftovers to make zesty, flavorful, delicious tacos in under 10 minutes. The recipe calls for some optional ingredients that you can use or substitute as you like. You can sauté the onions if you prefer—that would only require an oiled skillet and a hot plate.

1. Mix the chicken and salsa together in a microwave-safe bowl until the chicken is well coated.

2. Microwave on high for 15 seconds, stir, and cook for another 30 seconds.

3. For each of the 6 tortillas, add 3 tablespoons of chicken in the center and top with sour cream, cheese, and optional toppings.

CILANTRO-LIME CHICKEN

GLUTEN-FREE | SERVES: 3 | PREP TIME: **5 MINUTES** | COOK TIME: **20 MINUTES**

3 boneless, skinless chicken thighs, cut in half

3 tablespoons extra-virgin olive oil

1 lime, cut into 6 wedges

½ teaspoon chili powder

¼ teaspoon ground black pepper

¼ teaspoon salt

1 teaspoon brown sugar

1 tablespoon chopped fresh cilantro

Chicken thighs are amazing to work with. They are meaty, packed with flavor, and relatively cheap. You can make this dish with other boneless, skinless cuts of chicken, but chicken thighs are the cheapest. This recipe is very similar to the Lemon-Pepper Chicken (page 85), but the lime gives the chicken slightly more edge, especially in combination with the chili powder and cilantro. There is even a sweetness to this entrée that leaves you wanting more after every bite.

1. Preheat an oven or toaster oven to 400°F. Line a baking sheet with aluminum foil.

2. Place the chicken thigh pieces on the prepared baking sheet and brush them all over with the olive oil. Squeeze the juice from one lime wedge over each piece of chicken.

3. Combine the chili powder, pepper, and salt together in a small bowl, and sprinkle this mixture generously over the chicken thighs. Sprinkle the brown sugar over the chicken.

4. Bake for 20 minutes or until the chicken's internal temperature reaches 165°F.

5. Remove the chicken from the oven and serve topped with the cilantro.

Storage tip: Wrap leftover chicken in aluminum foil or seal it in an airtight container and refrigerate for up to 4 days.

CHEESY GROUND BEEF TACOS

GLUTEN-FREE | SERVES: 4 | PREP TIME: 5 MINUTES | COOK TIME: 15 MINUTES

1 pound ground beef

1 (1-ounce) packet taco seasoning

2/3 cup water

1/2 cup canned nacho cheese sauce

8 hard taco shells or corn tortillas

1/2 cup shredded iceberg lettuce

1/2 cup diced tomatoes, fresh or canned

1 ripe avocado, pitted and diced

Sour cream

1 lime, cut into wedges

This next-level taco adds a nacho twist in the way it melds the seasoned ground beef with nacho cheese before you even assemble the taco. Unlike the much simpler Shredded Chicken Street Tacos (page 86), which use cooked chicken, this recipe requires you to first cook the beef. It's worth the extra time, though, to attain that perfect beefy, cheesy, crunchy blend.

1. Place a skillet on your hot plate and set the hot plate to medium heat. Cook the ground beef in the skillet for about 6 minutes, stirring and breaking up the meat with a spoon, until it is completely browned. Pour the beef into a strainer set over a heatproof bowl to drain the grease from the skillet.

2. Return the beef to the skillet and set the skillet back on the hot plate over medium heat. Stir in the taco seasoning and water. Bring the mixture to a boil, then reduce the heat to medium-low and cook for 3 to 4 minutes or until the mixture has thickened. Stir in the nacho sauce and cook for another 5 minutes, stirring occasionally.

3. Add 2 tablespoons of beef mixture to each of the 8 taco shells. Top with lettuce, tomato, avocado, and sour cream. Squeeze a lime wedge over each taco for a pop of flavor.

Helpful hint: You can also squeeze the juice from the whole lime over the ground beef mixture when you add the cheese sauce.

Leftover tip: If you don't plan to make nachos later in the week, freeze your remaining nacho cheese sauce instead of refrigerating it. It lasts for 3 months in the freezer.

Storage tip: Make every day Taco Tuesday by cooking your ground beef ahead of time. Store it in a sealed container in the refrigerator for up to 4 days and build tacos in seconds anytime you please!

HONEY MUSTARD AND PRETZEL CHICKEN WITH RICE 🍞 🍳

2 cups water

1 cup uncooked white rice

3 boneless, skinless chicken thighs, cut in half

2 tablespoons extra-virgin olive oil

⅓ cup honey mustard

½ cup crushed pretzels

Storage tip: For easy microwave-able leftovers, chop up the chicken and combine it with the rice in an airtight container. Refrigerate for up to 4 days.

This chicken recipe has a lot of complexity but is very easy to make. The rich blend of flavors in this dish makes it one of my absolute favorite chicken meals. The pretzel crumbs add a nice crunch, and the combination of sweet, salty, and tangy is downright irresistible.

1. Preheat an oven or toaster oven to 400°F. Line a baking sheet with aluminum foil.

2. Bring the water to a boil in a saucepan on a hot plate set to high heat. Stir in the rice, return the water to a boil, then cover the saucepan and reduce the heat to low. Cook the rice for 20 minutes, until it is fluffy and most of the liquid is absorbed. Remove the pan from the heat.

3. While the rice cooks, place the chicken pieces on the prepared baking sheet. Brush the chicken all over with the olive oil and honey mustard, and sprinkle with the crushed pretzels. Bake for 20 minutes or until the chicken's internal temperature reaches 165°F.

4. Remove the chicken from the oven and cut two of the thigh pieces in half.

5. Divide the rice among 4 serving plates. Top each serving with 1½ pieces of chicken and enjoy.

DRESSED UP MEATBALLS

2 cups water

1 cup uncooked white rice

1 cup store-bought sweet-and-sour sauce

2 teaspoons soy sauce

1 carrot, peeled and cut into thin matchsticks

½ green bell pepper, seeded and chopped

1 teaspoon minced garlic

1 teaspoon onion powder

1 pound frozen precooked meatballs

One of my favorite ways to make a great, inexpensive, easy meal is to use precooked meat. Using precooked meat is a great way to utilize leftovers and, in this case, frozen meat, which may be cheaper than uncooked meat. Despite the cook time for the rice, this robust and flavorful meal comes together quickly and easily with minimal fuss.

1. Bring the water to a boil in a saucepan on a hot plate set to high heat. Stir in the rice, return the water to a boil, then cover the saucepan, reduce the heat to low, and cook for 20 minutes or until the rice is tender and most of the water has been absorbed.

2. When the rice has only 5 minutes left to cook, start preparing the meatballs. In a microwave-safe bowl, combine the sweet-and-sour sauce, soy sauce, carrots, bell pepper, garlic, and onion powder.

3. Add the frozen meatballs to the sauce mixture, cover loosely with a microwave-safe plate or plastic wrap (so that steam can escape), and microwave on high for 3 minutes.

4. Serve the meatballs with the rice.

Sub in: If you don't have fresh garlic, you can substitute it with ½ teaspoon garlic powder.

Storage tip: Store leftovers in separate sealed containers for 3 to 4 days in the refrigerator.

EASY MICROWAVE ENCHILADAS

GLUTEN-FREE | SERVES: **4** | PREP TIME: **5 MINUTES** | COOK TIME: **15 TO 20 MINUTES**

1 pound ground beef, or 3 cups shredded Slow-Cooker Whole Chicken (page 84) or store-bought rotisserie chicken

1 tablespoon taco seasoning (about ½ of a 1-ounce packet)

1 (19-ounce) can enchilada sauce, divided

Nonstick cooking spray

8 corn tortillas

1½ cups shredded Mexican-cheese blend

½ cup sour cream

3 tablespoons chopped fresh cilantro

These enchiladas are worth the extra effort, but they are still relatively easy to make. With four servings, this recipe is ideal for entertaining, or you can eat it throughout the week and save yourself some time.

1. If using ground beef, place a skillet on a hot plate set to medium heat. Cook the beef in the skillet for about 6 minutes, stirring and breaking it up with a spoon, until completely browned. Pour the beef into a strainer set over a heatproof bowl to drain the grease from the skillet.

2. Place the skillet back on the hot plate over medium heat and return the cooked beef to the skillet. If using shredded cooked chicken, on the hot plate set to medium heat. Mix in the taco seasoning, and cook for 1 to 2 minutes, until fragrant. Remove from the heat.

3. Pour the seasoned ground beef or chicken into a mixing bowl and add ½ cup of the enchilada sauce. Mix well.

4. Grease a microwave-safe baking dish with cooking spray and spread ½ cup of the enchilada sauce across the bottom of the dish.

5. Place 3 heaping tablespoons of the seasoned beef or chicken mixture onto one of the tortillas and roll tightly. Place the rolled tortilla in the prepared baking dish with the seam facing down. Repeat with the remaining meat and tortillas.

6. Pour the remaining enchilada sauce over the tortillas and top with the shredded cheese.

7. Microwave on high, uncovered, for 9 minutes.

8. Serve with sour cream and cilantro.

Sub in: If you don't have a Mexican-cheese blend, you can use shredded pepper jack or Cheddar cheese.

Helpful hint: If using cooked chicken instead of ground beef, start the recipe at step 2.

Storage tip: Cover leftovers in aluminum foil or store them in an airtight container in the refrigerator for up to 4 days.

TOMATO SOUP WITH GRILLED CHEESE CROUTONS

VEGETARIAN | SERVES **4** | PREP TIME: **5 MINUTES** | COOK TIME: **30 MINUTES**

FOR THE SOUP

2 tablespoons canola or vegetable oil

2 garlic cloves, minced

¼ cup chopped onion

1 (28-ounce) can stewed tomatoes

3 cups vegetable broth

¼ cup tomato paste

½ teaspoon ground black pepper

¼ cup milk

This scrumptious meal seems complicated, but it's worth the effort. The grilled cheese croutons are what make this flavorful meal such a treat. It's really nice to have the soup available in the refrigerator and be able to quickly add the croutons whenever you want that momentary return to childhood.

TO MAKE THE SOUP

1. Pour the oil into a saucepan or pot, put it on a hot plate, and set the hot plate to medium heat. When the oil is hot, add the garlic and cook just until it begins to turn golden brown, 1 to 2 minutes. Add the onion and cook until it is soft and translucent, about 6 minutes.

2. Add the stewed tomatoes, vegetable broth, tomato paste, and pepper and turn the heat to high. When the soup begins to boil, reduce the heat to low and let it simmer for 20 minutes. Remove from the heat and set aside.

3. Let the soup cool slightly, then carefully transfer the soup to the blender, filling it only about half way. Remove the center cap from the lid of the blender, cover the lid with a folded towel, and purée until smooth. Repeat with the remaining soup. Stir in the milk.

FOR THE GRILLED CHEESE CROUTONS

1 teaspoon butter, divided, plus more for the bread

4 slices bread

2 slices Cheddar cheese

TO MAKE THE GRILLED CHEESE CROUTONS

4. Butter one side of each slice of bread.

5. Place ½ teaspoon of butter in a skillet on a hot plate and set the hot plate to medium heat. When the butter is melted, place one slice of bread, butter-side down, in the hot skillet. Add a slice of cheese and top with another slice of bread, butter-side up. Cook the sandwich for 3 minutes, then use a spatula to check that the bottom of the sandwich is golden brown. Flip and cook for 2 more minutes. Transfer to a cutting board.

6. Add the remaining ½ teaspoon of butter to the skillet. Repeat step 5 with the remaining bread and cheese to make another grilled cheese sandwich.

7. On the cutting board, cut the sandwiches into small "croutons."

8. Serve the soup in bowls with the croutons on top.

Storage tip: Store the soup and croutons separately in air-tight containers in the refrigerator. It's okay to let the croutons get stale for some added crunch or to help them along by lightly toasting them.

Leftover tip: You can freeze leftover tomato paste for up to 3 months or use it to enhance the tomato flavor in other dishes you make.

95

SWEET-AND-SOUR CHICKEN

SERVES: **4** | PREP TIME: **10 MINUTES** | COOK TIME: **20 TO 25 MINUTES**

3 cups canola or vegetable oil

½ cup cornstarch

2 eggs

6 boneless, skinless chicken thighs, cut into 1-inch chunks

1 red bell pepper, seeded and cut into 1-inch chunks

1 green bell pepper, seeded and cut into 1-inch chunks

8 ounces store-bought sweet-and-sour sauce

Hot oil can be dangerous, so use caution when following this recipe. The safest way to make this is in an air fryer, if you have one. You can also bake the chicken according to the directions in the Honey Mustard and Pretzel Chicken recipe (page 90) or use a safer frying method by adapting the Orange Chicken with Snow Peas and Carrots recipe (page 106). If you are cooking in a dorm room, I do not recommend frying the chicken in oil.

1. Pour the canola oil into a high-sided skillet (the oil should be about 1½ inches deep), place it on your hot plate, and set the heat to medium.

2. Place the cornstarch in a gallon-size zip-top bag or similar size container with a tight-fitting lid.

3. In a medium bowl, beat the eggs.

4. Dip the chicken into the beaten eggs, then place it in the bag with the cornstarch. Seal the bag and shake to coat the chicken.

5. To test if the oil is ready, carefully place a small piece of chicken into the oil. If it bubbles, proceed to the next step.

6. Carefully place 5 pieces of chicken into the oil and cook for 3 to 4 minutes or until crispy and golden brown. Use tongs or a slotted spatula to transfer the chicken to a paper towel–lined plate and add 5 more pieces of chicken to the hot oil. Repeat until all the chicken is cooked.

7. Carefully pour the oil into another pot or heatproof bowl and return the skillet to the hot plate over medium heat. Add the bell peppers to the skillet and cook for 5 minutes or until they begin to soften. Stir in the sweet-and-sour sauce, cook for 3 more minutes, and then stir in the chicken. Stir until the chicken is glazed, then serve. Discard the frying oil.

Storage tip: Store leftovers in a sealed container for 3 to 4 days in the refrigerator.

CHICKEN AND
BROCCOLI ALFREDO

½ teaspoon salt, plus more for cooking pasta

2 tablespoons extra-virgin olive oil, divided

8 ounces (½ of a 1-pound box) dried penne pasta

2 cups frozen broccoli florets

3 tablespoons butter

1 cup heavy cream

Pinch ground black pepper

1½ cups grated Parmesan cheese

½ teaspoon garlic powder

1 cup shredded Slow-Cooker Whole Chicken (page 84) or store-bought rotisserie chicken

Adding chicken and some green vegetables to pasta makes all the difference. The dish becomes a well-rounded, hearty, and healthy yet simple meal that you can rely on over and over again.

1. Fill a large saucepan or pot with water, then add a few pinches of salt and 1 tablespoon of olive oil. Place the saucepan on your hot plate and set the hot plate to high heat. When the water comes to a boil, add the pasta and cook for 8 minutes.

2. After 8 minutes, add the broccoli to the boiling pasta. Cook for an additional 4 minutes, then drain the pasta and the broccoli in a strainer in the sink. Drizzle the pasta and broccoli with the remaining 1 tablespoon of olive oil and set aside.

3. Place the butter in a skillet on the hot plate and set the heat to medium. When the butter is melted, slowly add the cream, salt, and pepper, stirring constantly until the sauce begins to bubble. Add the Parmesan and garlic powder, stir well, then fold in the pasta and broccoli.

4. Mix in the chicken, cook until it's heated through, and serve.

With some spare dollars: Add a pinch of nutmeg to the sauce for some extra zing.

Storage tip: Leftovers will last about 3 days if kept refrigerated in a sealed container.

SLOPPY JOE GRILLED CHEESE SANDWICHES

SERVES: 4 | PREP TIME: 15 MINUTES | COOK TIME: 30 MINUTES

1 pound ground beef

1 (15-ounce) can sloppy joe sauce

8 teaspoons butter, divided

8 slices frozen Texas toast, thawed

8 slices Cheddar cheese

¼ teaspoon ground black pepper

Storage tip: The Texas toast holds up well to the sloppiness of this sandwich. Wrap leftover sandwiches in foil and store them in the refrigerator for a few days.

I love, love, love this recipe—melty cheesy goodness combined with the flavors and spices of sloppy joes. This recipe yields extra sandwiches and uses up the sloppy joe mix and ground beef all at once. That's perfect, because you'll want more.

1. Place a skillet on a hot plate and set the hot plate to medium heat. When the skillet is hot, add the beef and cook, breaking up the meat with a spoon or spatula, until it is completely browned, about 6 minutes.

2. Pour the beef into a strainer set over a heatproof bowl to drain the grease from the skillet, then return the cooked meat to the skillet on the hot plate. Add the sloppy joe sauce and cook according to the instructions on the can. Scrape the ground beef mixture into a heatproof bowl and set aside.

3. Wipe out the skillet, place 2 teaspoons of butter in it, and return it to the hot plate over medium heat. When the butter melts, place 1 slice of bread in the hot skillet. Add 2 slices of cheese and one-quarter of the sloppy joe beef, then top with another slice of bread. Cook the sandwich for 3 minutes, then use a spatula to check that the bottom of the sandwich is golden brown. Flip and cook for 2 minutes.

4. Use a spatula to transfer the sandwich to a plate. Repeat step 3 until all the sandwiches are cooked.

CHICKEN TORTILLA SOUP 🍳

GLUTEN-FREE | SERVES: **4** | PREP TIME: **5 MINUTES** | COOK TIME: **1 HOUR**

4 cups chicken broth

2 cups shredded Slow-Cooker Whole Chicken (page 84) or store-bought rotisserie chicken

1 (10-ounce) can diced tomatoes and green chilies

1 (15-ounce) can sweet corn, drained

1 (15-ounce) can black beans, drained and rinsed

½ teaspoon ground black pepper

1 tablespoon garlic powder

Juice of 1 lime

⅓ cup crushed tortilla chips (check label for gluten-free)

You can enjoy this recipe as a starter or as a whole meal. The chicken makes it a very hearty dinner. The cook time is quite long, but you don't have to do anything to it. It's just like using a slow cooker. You could speed up the cook time by adding heat, but for the best results, you want the flavors to mingle and bond as much as possible. It's well worth the wait when you get that perfect bite of chewy, crunchy, and zesty soup.

1. Pour the chicken broth into a large saucepan or pot and place it on a hot plate set to medium heat. When it starts to simmer (steaming with bubbles just beginning to rise to the surface), mix in the chicken, diced tomatoes and green chilies, corn, black beans, pepper, garlic powder, and lime juice. Cover, reduce the heat to medium-low, and simmer for 1 hour.

2. Remove the pan from the heat and ladle the soup into cups or bowls. Top with crushed tortilla chips.

With some spare dollars: You can buy tortilla strips in the salad section of the grocery store to use instead of the tortilla chips. They're a bit expensive but will make for a more authentic tortilla soup.

SLOW-COOKER
SPAGHETTI MARINARA

VEGETARIAN | SERVES: 4 | PREP TIME: 5 MINUTES | COOK TIME: 6 HOURS 20 MINUTES

1 (15-ounce) can diced tomatoes

1 (24-ounce) jar spaghetti or marinara sauce

1 teaspoon onion powder

1 teaspoon chopped fresh basil

1 teaspoon ground black pepper

1 cup water

8 ounces (½ of a 1-pound box) dried spaghetti pasta, broken in half

Here is another great recipe worth waiting for. It's so easy to put together, and all you have to do is let it sit for about six hours. This is the perfect dinner to start preparing before you head off to a three-hour class or a short work shift because you can throw it together and let the slow cooker do all the work of creating this amazing sauce. Another plus with this recipe is there is enough to share, so it's an easy-to-use recipe for date night as well.

1. In a slow cooker, combine the diced tomatoes, spaghetti sauce, onion powder, basil, pepper, and water. Cook on low for 6 hours.

2. Stir in the spaghetti and cook on high for 20 minutes or until the pasta reaches your desired doneness.

With some spare dollars: Make spaghetti and meatballs easily by adding precooked frozen meatballs to the slow cooker after you add the dried pasta.

Storage tip: You can keep leftovers in the refrigerator for a few days in a sealed container. To make the pasta spring back to life, add a dollop of butter or margarine when you reheat it in the microwave.

101

SUPER-CHEESY LASAGNA

VEGETARIAN | SERVES 4 | PREP TIME: 5 MINUTES | COOK TIME: 12 MINUTES

1 (16-ounce) container ricotta cheese

½ cup grated Parmesan cheese, divided

2 teaspoons salt

1 teaspoon ground black pepper

1 cup store-bought marinara sauce, divided

1 (9-ounce) box oven-ready lasagna noodles

2 cups shredded low-moisture mozzarella cheese

Storage tip: Cover leftover lasagna with aluminum foil and store it in refrigerator for up to 5 days.

Lasagna is one of the best things you can have as a college student. It's robust and hearty. Plus, it keeps well and tastes even better a few days after you've made it—and this version couldn't be easier to make!

1. In a bowl, mix together the ricotta, 2 tablespoons of the Parmesan cheese, the salt, and pepper. Set aside.

2. In the bottom of an 8-by-8-inch microwave-safe dish, spread ⅓ cup of the marinara sauce. Top the sauce with a layer of lasagna noodles, breaking up the noodles as needed to fit them in a single layer. Use a spatula or spoon to spread half of the ricotta mixture on top of the lasagna noodles, then sprinkle on one-third of the mozzarella.

3. Repeat the layers with another ⅓ cup of marinara sauce, another layer of noodles, the remaining ricotta mixture, and half of the remaining mozzarella cheese. Finish with the remaining ⅓ cup of marinara sauce, the remaining noodles, and the rest of the mozzarella.

4. Top with the remaining Parmesan cheese and cook in the microwave on high heat for 12 minutes or until the cheese is melted.

With some spare dollars: Add to the flavor of the ricotta filling by mixing in ½ teaspoon each of onion powder and garlic powder.

THAI-INSPIRED PEANUT NOODLES

VEGETARIAN | SERVES 2 | PREP TIME: 5 MINUTES | COOK TIME: 5 MINUTES

2 packages instant ramen noodles, seasoning packets discarded or saved for another use

½ cup Peanut Sauce (page 56)

2 tablespoons shredded carrots

1 tablespoon chopped fresh cilantro

2 tablespoons peanuts

This recipe is one of my favorite meals to make on the fly. It is super simple and so impressive. The peanut sauce —used in other recipes as well—is really easy to prepare with very basic ingredients. This dish uses ramen noodles, so this recipe is a really exciting way to jazz up a cheap meal.

1. In a saucepan on a hot plate, cook both pads of ramen together following the package instructions, doubling the amount of water.

2. Drain the noodles and transfer them to a bowl with the peanut sauce. Add the carrots, cilantro, and peanuts. Toss well before serving.

Storage tip: Store any leftovers in a sealed container in the refrigerator for up to 1 week.

103

SEARED STEAK WITH MUSHROOMS AND BROWNED BUTTER

GLUTEN-FREE | SERVES **2** | PREP TIME: **10 MINUTES** | COOK TIME: **10 MINUTES**

FOR THE MUSHROOMS

1 tablespoon
   extra-virgin
   olive oil

1 (8-ounce)
   package of white
   mushrooms,
   trimmed
   and sliced

1 teaspoon garlic
   powder

Salt

Ground black
   pepper

This hearty entrée works great with Rosemary-Garlic Potatoes (page 50) as a side. It's also surprisingly affordable because it uses an inexpensive cut of steak. Not all steak dinners have to drain your bank account. Like going to the deli, asking your butcher for just what you want is a great way to save money and avoid waste. Use two petite filets and enjoy this meal with a companion.

TO MAKE THE MUSHROOMS

1. Heat the oil in a skillet on a hot plate set to medium heat. Add the mushrooms, garlic powder, and a pinch each of salt and pepper. Cook for 3 minutes, stirring frequently, until the mushrooms are tender.

2. Transfer the mushrooms to two plates and return the skillet to the hot plate set to medium heat.

FOR THE STEAK

2 petite filets, at room temperature

½ teaspoon salt, divided

½ teaspoon ground black pepper, divided

½ teaspoon garlic powder, divided

3 tablespoons butter

TO MAKE THE STEAKS

3. Season both steaks on one side with ¼ teaspoon of salt, ¼ teaspoon of pepper, and ¼ teaspoon of garlic powder, then carefully place the steaks in the skillet, seasoned-side down.

4. Sprinkle the remaining ¼ teaspoon of salt, ¼ teaspoon of pepper, and ¼ teaspoon of garlic powder on top of both steaks. Let them cook for 1 minute, then add the butter to the skillet and cook for 1 more minute, scooping the butter over the steaks with a spoon as it melts.

5. Flip the steaks and continue to baste them with butter for 1 minute or until the steaks reach desired doneness: 135°F for medium-rare, 145°F for medium, or 160°F for well-done.

6. Use a spatula to remove the steaks from the skillet and place them on top of the mushrooms on the individual serving plates. Stir the butter constantly in the skillet over medium heat for about 1 more minute or until the butter becomes brown and frothy. Remove the skillet from the heat and pour the browned butter over the steak and mushrooms.

ORANGE CHICKEN WITH SNOW PEAS AND CARROTS

GLUTEN-FREE | SERVES **4** | PREP TIME: **5 MINUTES** | COOK TIME: **15 MINUTES**

2 tablespoons
sesame oil

2 tablespoons
extra-virgin
olive oil

1 pound boneless,
skinless chicken
thighs, cut into
1-inch pieces

1 (14-ounce) bag
coleslaw mix

½ cup soy sauce
(check label for
gluten-free)

1 teaspoon garlic
powder

Ground black
pepper

1 cup fresh
snow peas

1 (20-ounce)
can mandarin
oranges, drained

1 tablespoon
honey

This healthy Asian-inspired recipe offers complexity and great flavors with minimal effort. Making this meal consists mostly of tossing ingredients into the pan at one point or another. You get four meals out of this dish, which makes it perfect for entertaining or for prepping future meals.

1. Place the sesame oil and olive oil in a skillet on a hot plate and set the hot plate to medium heat.

2. When the oils are hot, add the chicken to the skillet and cook, stirring occasionally, for 5 minutes or until the chicken is cooked through.

3. Stir in the coleslaw mix, soy sauce, garlic powder, and pepper to taste. Cook for 5 minutes, stirring frequently, until the vegetables begin to soften.

4. Stir in the snow peas and cook for an additional 2 minutes, then turn off the heat and stir in the mandarin oranges and honey. Serve hot.

Storage tip: You can store leftovers in an airtight container in the refrigerator for up to 4 days.

Leftover tip: Snow peas freeze well and are very versatile. You can incorporate them into noodles, salads, and soups for some extra flavor and nutrients.

Sesame oil is a key ingredient in many Asian-inspired dishes, and it stores well for a very long time. Keep leftover sesame oil on hand with your olive oil and vegetable oil.

BEEF CHILI

1 tablespoon extra-virgin olive oil

1 pound ground beef

2½ tablespoons chili powder

1 teaspoon onion powder

1 tablespoon garlic powder

1 tablespoon ground cumin

2 tablespoons sugar

3 tablespoons tomato paste

Chili can be very nuanced, and creating a chili with a deep, rich flavor is challenging. This recipe provides a very good starting point, and it demystifies chili so that you can get great flavors without overcomplicating the process. Many of these ingredients should be in your cupboard already.

1. Place a large saucepan or pot on a hot plate and set the hot plate to medium heat.

2. When the pan is hot, put in the oil and ground beef and cook, stirring frequently and breaking it up into pieces, for 4 to 5 minutes or until browned.

3. Pour the beef into a strainer set over a heatproof bowl to drain the grease from the pan. Return the beef to the saucepan and add the chili powder, onion powder, garlic powder, cumin, sugar, tomato paste, salt, and pepper. Stir well, then add the beef broth, diced tomatoes, kidney beans, and tomato sauce.

1 teaspoon salt

½ teaspoon ground black pepper

½ cup beef broth

1 (15-ounce) can diced tomatoes

1 (15-ounce) can red kidney beans, drained and rinsed

1 (8-ounce) can tomato sauce

4. Bring the mixture to a boil, then reduce the heat to low and simmer uncovered for 20 minutes, stirring occasionally.

With some spare dollars: You can add creaminess to the chili by adding a tablespoon of sour cream to each bowl.

Storage tip: Refrigerate leftovers in a sealed container for up to 4 days. This chili can be served with rice, pasta, cornbread, tortilla chips, or hot dogs. Get creative with it!

Leftover tip: Need to use up your leftover tomato paste? Make Tomato Soup with Grilled Cheese Croutons (page 94).

109

GREEK GYRO SKILLET

GLUTEN-FREE | SERVES: **6** | PREP TIME: **10 MINUTES** | COOK TIME: **25 MINUTES**

1 tablespoon extra-virgin olive oil

1 pound ground chicken

1 small zucchini, trimmed and sliced (about 1 cup)

3 teaspoons Greek seasoning blend

½ teaspoon garlic powder

½ teaspoon onion powder

½ teaspoon salt

½ teaspoon ground black pepper

1 quart chicken broth

2 cups uncooked white rice

⅓ cup chopped pitted black olives

⅓ cup crumbled feta cheese

This recipe is nice to have on hand when you need something that's a little bit different but still very accessible. This skillet meal is inspired by Greek gyros and incorporates as much of that flavor as possible. This recipe calls for chicken, but you can substitute another protein. Just remember to drain the fat out of meats that aren't as lean.

1. Place the oil in a skillet on a hot plate and set the hot plate to medium heat.

2. When the oil is hot, add the ground chicken to the skillet. Stir, breaking into crumbles, and cook until the chicken is fully cooked, about 6 minutes. Add the zucchini, then stir in the Greek seasoning, garlic powder, onion powder, salt, and pepper. Cook for 4 minutes or until the zucchini is softened, stirring occasionally.

3. Add the chicken broth to the skillet and bring the mixture to a gentle boil.

4. Stir in the rice, reduce the heat to low, cover the pan, and cook for 15 minutes or until the broth is absorbed and the rice is tender.

5. When the rice is done cooking, remove the pan from the heat. (If the rice is still not tender, re-cover the pot and continue to simmer for another 5 minutes).

6. Stir in the olives and feta before serving.

Storage tip: This recipe will keep for up to 4 days in the refrigerator if you store it in a sealed container.

Leftover tip: Feta is an excellent ingredient to sprinkle on salads and pastas. You can even add it to a sandwich.

Streusel-Topped Coffee Cake
In A Mug P.122

6

For the Sweet Tooth

I carried a sweet tooth with me through my college years, and I still love a sweet treat at any time of day, especially after dinner or in the afternoon. These are some of my favorite easy desserts that you can whip up in an instant and enjoy throughout the week.

BIRTHDAY CAKE IN A MUG

VEGETARIAN | SERVES: **1** | PREP TIME: **5 MINUTES** | COOK TIME: **2 MINUTES**

4 tablespoons
all-purpose flour

4 tablespoons
sugar

½ teaspoon
baking powder

3 tablespoons milk

1 tablespoon
canola or
vegetable oil

1 tablespoon
vanilla extract

1 tablespoon
rainbow sprinkles

There is never a bad time to make a birthday cake, especially when you can make one easily in your coffee mug. The convenience of this dessert makes it a really fun, informal way to celebrate your birthday or a friend's. You can even use a personalized mug to make this a gift. Either way, this easy-to-make dessert can brighten up any special occasion. I also like the fact that it can be prepared without a lot of forethought, making it a great last-minute gesture or a spur-of-the-moment sweet treat.

1. In a large, microwave-safe mug, combine the flour, sugar, baking powder, milk, oil, vanilla extract, and sprinkles. Mix well, then microwave on high for 2 minutes.

2. Remove from the microwave and let cool for 2 minutes before eating.

With some spare dollars: Add a spread of your choice to ice the cake. A good—and more functional—substitute for icing is a can of whipped cream. Swirl it over the top to finish the cake.

Leftover tip: If you have leftover sprinkles, don't sweat it. They stay good for 5 years, and you can incorporate them into so many desserts.

114

CHOCOLATE AND
PEANUT BUTTER COOKIE

VEGETARIAN | SERVES: 1 | PREP TIME: 5 MINUTES | COOK TIME: 55 SECONDS

1 tablespoon butter, at room temperature

1 tablespoon brown sugar

1 teaspoon granulated sugar

Splash vanilla extract

Pinch baking powder

1 tablespoon water

2 teaspoons cocoa powder

1 tablespoon all-purpose flour

1 tablespoon mini chocolate chips

1 tablespoon creamy peanut butter

Chocolate and peanut butter is a classic combination, so this cookie recipe is an ace up your sleeve. It's one of the ultimate flavor profiles and so easy to make. My favorite thing about this cookie is that it is a perfect single-serve treat. For those occasions when you want something sweet but don't want to overdo it, this recipe is right there for a quick and tasty pick-me-up. It also makes a nice sweet bite you can enjoy on the go and a delicious way to finish off a meal. This cookie especially complements meals that incorporate peanut sauce.

1. Place the butter in a large, microwave-safe mug and microwave it for 25 seconds or until melted.

2. Remove the mug from the microwave. Stir in the brown sugar, granulated sugar, vanilla, and baking powder, then add the water, cocoa powder, and flour. Mix until well combined. Fold in the chocolate chips. Microwave on high for 30 seconds.

3. Remove the mug from the microwave and invert the cookie onto a plate. Spread the top with peanut butter, let cool for 2 minutes, then enjoy.

Leftover tip: You can make an easy hot chocolate mix out of leftover cocoa powder. Just mix in 1 tablespoon of sugar for every 2 tablespoons of cocoa and add a pinch of salt. Stir 3 tablespoons of the mix into 8 ounces of hot water or milk.

BERRY CRUMBLE

VEGETARIAN | SERVES: **1** | PREP TIME: **2 MINUTES** | COOK TIME: **2 MINUTES**

1 tablespoon butter

¼ cup quick-cooking oats

¾ cup frozen berries, thawed

1 teaspoon sugar

½ teaspoon cornstarch

The berry crumble is another classic recipe that you should keep as a standard go-to for particular meals. Desserts often work well on their own, but they can also be carefully selected as a key piece of an entire meal. The berry crumble is the strongest dessert in that it is potentially the most versatile. Depending on your entrée, berries may be the best way to cap off the experience. I also won't say I never made this for breakfast. This recipe can use up any leftover berries you have from the Vanilla Yogurt and Berry Parfait (page 30).

1. In a small, microwave-safe bowl, microwave the butter for 25 seconds or until melted. Add the oats and mix until they are completely coated in the butter.

2. In a large, microwave-safe mug, mix together the berries, sugar, and cornstarch. Scoop the oat mixture on top of the berry mixture and spread it out evenly.

3. Microwave on high for 90 seconds or until the berries are bubbling. (If the berries are not bubbling, microwave for another 30 seconds.)

4. Let cool for 2 minutes before eating.

Sub in: You can use a packet of flavored oatmeal instead of the quick oats to add complexity to your berry crumble. You can't go wrong with maple and brown sugar or cinnamon-apple.

Leftover tip: Cornstarch has no determined shelf life, so you can hold on to the same can indefinitely. It also has numerous uses for thickening up different types of foods. If you really want to, you can even use it to scrub your pots and pans and clean your cooktop as the granules are naturally abrasive.

EASY MICROWAVE BROWNIE

VEGETARIAN | SERVES: **1** | PREP TIME: **2 MINUTES** | COOK TIME: **80 SECONDS**

¼ cup granulated sugar

3 tablespoons cocoa powder

2 tablespoons canola or vegetable oil

¼ cup water

2 tablespoons brown sugar

Pinch salt

¼ cup all-purpose flour

3 tablespoons chocolate chips

Splash vanilla extract

If there is one dessert that doubles as a convenient snack, it's brownies. This again is where the single-serve aspect is genius because I would eat a whole plate of brownies without even thinking about it. Whether I'm in the zone, studying for a test, or binge-watching my favorite show (or catching up on the gossip about my favorite show while I'm supposed to be studying for a test), I can avoid the awkwardness of demolishing a whole plate of brownies by making myself this compact treat instead. It also goes great with ice cream. One of my favorite things about this recipe is how minimal the instructions are. It's one of the easiest things to cook, so the payoff is richer, and, if you want, you can easily go back and make that second brownie.

1. In a large, microwave-safe mug, whisk together the granulated sugar, cocoa powder, oil, water, brown sugar, and salt. Stir in the flour, chocolate chips, and vanilla extract.

2. Microwave on high for 80 seconds.

3. Remove from the microwave and let cool for 2 minutes before eating.

MOLTEN CHOCOLATE CAKE

VEGETARIAN | SERVES: **1** | PREP TIME: **5 MINUTES** | COOK TIME: **90 SECONDS**

¼ cup all-purpose flour

1 teaspoon baking powder

2 tablespoons sugar

2 tablespoons cocoa powder

Pinch salt

2 tablespoons canola or vegetable oil

2 tablespoons milk

Splash vanilla extract

2 tablespoons chocolate chips

One nice thing about desserts is that a lot of the ingredients are the same and most of them are shelf-stable, which means you can keep them in a cupboard, or any convenient space, for a pretty long time. Still, you might shy away from making desserts because baking can take a lot of time, especially if you are waiting for an oven to preheat. However, that problem is quickly solved with a microwave. Another problem, also solved by the microwave, is that you may not have access to an oven. That's why these single-serve desserts are such a nice solution. They are fast and simple recipes that use common ingredients, so you aren't having to buy a lot every time you want something sweet. This recipe adds a chocolatey flourish that sets it apart.

1. In a large, microwave-safe mug, mix together the flour, baking powder, sugar, cocoa powder, and salt. Then stir in the oil, milk, and vanilla. Drop the chocolate chips into the center of the batter.

2. Microwave on high for 90 seconds.

CHOCOLATE CHIP COOKIE BARS

VEGETARIAN | SERVES: **3** | PREP TIME: **5 MINUTES** | COOK TIME: **4 MINUTES**

4 tablespoons butter plus more for greasing

⅓ cup packed brown sugar

1 egg

2 teaspoons milk

Splash vanilla extract

¼ teaspoon baking powder

Pinch salt

½ cup all-purpose flour

½ cup chocolate chips

These technically serve three people or should last you for three separate meals, but let's be real—these are going down your gullet before they even cool off. It's a good thing they're easy to make. This recipe calls for a microwave-safe dish, but you can make them on a plate if you don't mind the curvature that results from the dough cooking along the rim.

1. Place the butter in a medium-size, microwave-safe bowl and microwave on high for 15 seconds or until it has softened.

2. Remove the bowl from the microwave, add the brown sugar, and stir until combined. Mix in the egg, milk, and vanilla, then add the baking powder, salt, and flour. Mix until well combined. Stir in the chocolate chips.

3. Grease a microwave-safe baking dish and pour in the batter, smoothing the top.

4. Microwave on high for 3 minutes, using the turntable. If your microwave does not have a turntable, microwave for 1 minute at a time, moving the dish one-quarter turn after each minute.

5. Remove from the microwave and let cool for 5 minutes before cutting and serving.

With some spare dollars: Add crushed walnuts to this recipe to give the cookie bars more flavor and texture.

VANILLA SPRINKLE COOKIES

VEGETARIAN | YIELD: **6 COOKIES** | PREP TIME: **5 MINUTES** | COOK TIME: **10 MINUTES**

½ cup all-purpose flour

½ teaspoon baking powder

Pinch salt

⅓ cup sugar

1 tablespoon unsalted butter, at room temperature

1 egg

Splash vanilla extract

⅓ cup rainbow sprinkles

What I adore about this recipe is that it's done in the toaster oven. Microwaves are super convenient and fast, but a toaster oven gives the cookies a more authentic baked taste. Because these are so sweet, a few go a long way, so I also enjoy that these last a little bit longer. You can even stretch them out for a week.

1. Preheat an oven or toaster oven to 375°F. Line a baking sheet with aluminum foil.

2. In a bowl, mix together the flour, baking powder, and salt.

3. In a separate bowl, mix together the sugar and butter until well combined. Add the egg and vanilla and stir. Add the flour mixture to the bowl and mix until well combined. Fold in the sprinkles.

4. Roll the dough into 6 equal-size balls, about 1 tablespoon each, and place them on the prepared baking sheet.

5. Bake for 9 minutes, then remove the cookies from the oven and let them rest for an additional 5 minutes before serving.

Helpful hint: If you have a regular-size oven and prefer to use it, preheat the oven to 375°F before starting and follow the rest of the instructions.

STREUSEL-TOPPED COFFEE CAKE IN A MUG

VEGETARIAN | SERVES: **1** | PREP TIME: **5 MINUTES** | COOK TIME: **2 MINUTES**

FOR THE CAKE

2 tablespoons butter

2 tablespoons sugar

⅓ cup all-purpose flour

¼ teaspoon baking powder

¼ teaspoon ground cinnamon

¼ cup milk

Splash vanilla extract

This is another amazing dessert recipe to have in your arsenal. Even more than the Berry Crumble (page 116), this dessert is uniquely qualified to enjoy as a breakfast treat as well. Have it with coffee as a morning or afternoon pick-me-up. Another thing I love about this recipe is that the streusel can be used on other desserts. You can top your berry crumble with it to add another layer of flavor and texture. You can also incorporate berries into this recipe to add flavor and texture to the coffee cake. With or without berries, this recipe offers that cinnamon-sugar combo you can't do without.

TO MAKE THE CAKE BATTER

In a large, microwave-safe mug, microwave the butter for 10 to 20 seconds or until melted. Add the sugar, flour, baking powder, and cinnamon. Mix well. Stir in the milk and vanilla.

FOR THE STREUSEL

1 tablespoon butter, at room temperature

2 tablespoons all-purpose flour

1 tablespoon brown sugar

¼ teaspoon ground cinnamon

Splash vanilla extract

TO MAKE THE STREUSEL

1. In a small bowl, mix together the butter, flour, brown sugar, cinnamon, and vanilla.

2. Spread the streusel topping over the cake batter in the mug and microwave on high for 90 seconds.

3. Remove from microwave and let cool 2 minutes before eating.

WHITE CHOCOLATE AND LIME MINI CHEESECAKES

NO-COOK, VEGETARIAN | SERVES: 6 | PREP TIME: 10 MINUTES, PLUS 4 HOURS TO CHILL

FOR THE CRUST

¾ cup crushed graham crackers

1 tablespoon sugar

3 tablespoons unsalted butter, at room temperature

This dessert is delicious and simple to make. However, you will need to be patient to enjoy it. There is no cooking involved, but the cheesecake needs to firm up in the refrigerator for a few hours before it's ready. It's totally worth the wait, and it's a brilliant treat to share at the end of the day with roommates or guests.

TO MAKE THE CRUST

1. In a small bowl, mix the graham crackers, sugar, and butter until combined.

2. Pour the crust mixture evenly into a 6-cup muffin tin and press the crust down with a spoon.

FOR THE FILLING

12 ounces cream cheese, at room temperature

¼ cup sugar

½ teaspoon vanilla extract

3 tablespoons freshly squeezed lime juice

4 teaspoons lime zest

½ cup whipped cream

3 tablespoons white chocolate chips

TO MAKE THE FILLING

3. Use the mixing bowl again to combine the cream cheese, sugar, vanilla, lime juice, and lime zest to create a smooth mixture.

4. Once smooth, mix in the whipped cream and white choco-late chips, then spoon evenly into the prepared muffin tin.

5. Refrigerate for at least 4 hours to allow the mixture to become firm.

Helpful hint: For a smoother texture, use a microwave to melt the white chocolate.

Leftover tip: Add leftover cream cheese and black pepper to taste to a pot of canned corn for a delicious, creamy side dish.

CHERRY PIE CUPS

VEGETARIAN | SERVES: **6** | PREP TIME: **LESS THAN 5 MINUTES** |
COOK TIME: **10 MINUTES**

Nonstick cooking spray or butter, for greasing the muffin tin

1 refrigerated pie crust, at room temperature

1 (21-ounce) can cherry pie filling

Sometimes you want a sweet treat in the middle of your day or something small after dinner. These delicious little cherry pies are just the right thing for when your sweet tooth strikes. They are incredibly easy to make and irresistible once you have them in your refrigerator. Try to make them last the week, or you may need to bake some extra batches so that they don't disappear too fast.

1. Preheat an oven or toaster oven to 425°F. Lightly grease a 6-cup muffin tin with nonstick cooking spray or butter.

2. Roll out the pie dough, then cut out 6 (4-inch) rounds, using the rim of a mug or pint glass, and place the rounds in the muffin tin, pressing firmly to shape.

3. Add 3 tablespoons of cherry pie filling to each of the cups. Bake for about 10 minutes, or until the crust is golden brown.

Helpful hint: You'll have pie filling left over, which is perfect for a sundae. With the six cherry pie cups, that's seven desserts total—one for every night of the week!

MEASUREMENT CONVERSIONS

VOLUME EQUIVALENTS (LIQUID)

US Standard	US Standard (ounces)	Metric (approximate)
2 tablespoons	1 fl. oz.	30 mL
¼ cup	2 fl. oz.	60 mL
½ cup	4 fl. oz.	120 mL
1 cup	8 fl. oz.	240 mL
1½ cups	12 fl. oz.	355 mL
2 cups or 1 pint	16 fl. oz.	475 mL
4 cups or 1 quart	32 fl. oz.	1 L
1 gallon	128 fl. oz.	4 L

GLOSSARY

BASTE: To pour juices over meat while cooking in order to keep it from drying out

FOLD: To gently combine an ingredient into a mixture by spooning the mix up and over to cover it up

MINCE: To grind or cut an ingredient, such as garlic, into very fine pieces

SAUTÉ: To quickly fry an ingredient, such as onions or mushrooms, in a greased pan

SEAR: To burn the surface of a food or char it, usually relating to meat

SEASON: To add or improve flavor by enhancing food with herbs, spices, or other condiments

SIMMER: To cook liquid just below the boiling point and keep it in that state

ZEST: Shavings from the peel of a citrus fruit such as a lemon or an orange

INDEX

131

133

134

136

137

138

139

ACKNOWLEDGMENTS

Thank you to my husband, Eric, for his constant support, and to my parents, John and Elizabeth, for their help with the children and for turning our full house into a test kitchen to make this cookbook possible. I would not have been able to write this book if it weren't for my amazing followers and the new generations of shoppers who are discovering my blog. Thank you all for reading, watching, and cooking with me.

ABOUT THE AUTHOR

Sara Lundberg is a wife and proud mother of four incredible children under four years old. After graduating from the University of Southern California, she created her blog BudgetSavvyDiva.com in 2009 to help shoppers be smart with their budgets and make inexpensive meals that feed a family. Sara's philosophy is that you don't have to pass up great style and awesome food to save money. You just have to be savvy. Sara's passion for making exceptional food and her background in retail management and internet marketing give her unique insight that helps her lead hundreds of thousands of followers on a budget-savvy journey.

CPSIA information can be obtained
at www.ICGtesting.com
Printed in the USA
JSHW010545280620
6374JS00005B/22

9 781646 116744